JOIE WARNER'S

take a tin of tuna

JOIE WARNER'S

take a tin of tuna

65 inspired recipes *for* every
meal of *the* day

PHOTOGRAPHS BY DREW WARNER

CHRONICLE BOOKS
SAN FRANCISCO

Text, recipes, and photographs copyright © 2004 by Flavor Publications, Inc.

Library of Congress Cataloging-in-Publication Data available.

ISBN 0-8118-3542-1

Manufactured in China.

Design and illustrations
  by Lesley Feldman
Prop and food styling
  by Drew and Joie Warner

Distributed in Canada by
Raincoast Books
9050 Shaughnessy Street
Vancouver, British Columbia
V6P 6E5

10 9 8 7 6 5 4 3 2 1

Chronicle Books LLC
85 Second Street
San Francisco, California
94105

www.chroniclebooks.com

page 2: Tuna-Anchovy Puffs, page 37.

acknowledgments

First and foremost, a big thank you to my darling Drew for his gorgeous photography (canned tuna never looked so good!), and especially for creating the charming "school of fish" photo just for me. Your extraordinary photographs, design talents, and dedication to perfection make my recipes look beautiful and as delicious as they taste.

Thanks also to my terrific team of tuna tasters and testers: Susan Allen, Sarah Best, Lucy and Sou Chang, Sharee Fiore, Michael Green, Meredith Jones, Rikki Klein, Louise and Thom Northrop, Linda and Dan Schwartz, and Debbi and Jay Zuckerman. I just wish all of you were as enthusiastic about doing the dishes!

Another big thank you to Bill LeBlond for your enthusiasm for *Take a Tin of Tuna*. The list would not be complete without thanking the rest of the crew at Chronicle Books: assistant editors Amy Treadwell and Holly Burrows and art director Azi Rad, for all your hard work and for listening to and using many of my suggestions. You were all wonderful to work with on this project.

Thanks also to Lesley Feldman for her fun illustrations and fine design, to Margaret Jackson and Miss Molly for your help in the very beginning, and, finally, a big hug to Mom for always being there.

table *of* contents

At right: Tuscan Tuna, Celery, and White Bean Salad, page 81

introduction

Believe it! There's a whole lot more you can do with a tin of TUNA than fix a quick TUNA sandwich or make a TUNA casserole! Yes, these all-American favorites can be very appealing when prepared with care, but there's a big, wide world of recipes out there, mostly from the Mediterranean, where cooks treat canned TUNA as a delicacy, not just an everyday convenience food.

First, let's look at the facts: Almost every kitchen in America—and that probably includes yours—has at least one tin of tuna on the shelf at all times. (Actually, it's America's favorite fish—95 percent of it canned.) And it's no wonder. It's one of the few foods that's really good in a can—plus it's easy on the pocketbook, and it doesn't need cooking! We Americans consume millions of cans of the stuff every week, making it one of the top staples in the American kitchen. (Unfortunately, most of it ends up mashed with mayonnaise and celery and sandwiched between two slices of fluffy white bread.) Its popularity, no doubt, is due to its taste—it's a fish that tastes a lot like chicken (and without all those pesky little bones!), hence its charming moniker, "chicken of the sea."

Now, you'd think, with all the canned tuna eaten in this country, that home cooks would feel compelled to explore more interesting and adventurous ways to prepare it. Well, I'm one of those cooks and, over the years,

I've become more and more inspired to write this book, especially since I've found no other books on the subject—nothing at all to encourage people to try different ideas.

So here's my compendium of tempting, full-flavored, zesty, and mouthwatering recipes to start your taste buds tingling: everything from soups, appetizers, and entrées to salads, sandwiches, and then some. You'll soon discover that "ordinary" canned tuna can taste quite extraordinary. I've created a variety of recipes for everything from France's famous salade Niçoise to Spanish tapas—with stops along the way for a terrific tuna melt and (yes!) good old-fashioned tuna casserole, this time with a slightly new twist. I've included several ways to serve canned tuna as antipasti. Or try it in a cheese soufflé or even in a smooth and creamy fondue. Tuna, lemon, and capers tossed with pasta and accompanied with a salad and crusty bread is good enough for company. The same goes for savory Risotto with Tuna and Tomatoes or elegant and easy Chicken Tonnato. Looking for a lunch dish? I've included a splendid Italian recipe for tuna-stuffed peppers. Or there's Tuna Quiche with Broccoli and Sweet Red Pepper (or make mini quiche tartlets to serve as appetizers) or Cream Cheese and Tuna Pâté.

I've also included tips for buying and storing tuna, plus a list of tuna-friendly pantry items to keep on hand so it's always easy to whip up delicious impromptu meals for family and friends. To top it off, the recipes are quick and simple to prepare and—most important—full of palate-pleasing flavor.

Canned tuna may never be hip or chic—you'd have a hard time finding it gracing the menus of trendy restaurants around town. (Perhaps they'll soon catch on, since Mediterranean dishes featuring tinned tuna are surprisingly sophisticated.) And please ignore the food snobs who turn up their noses at anything canned and will try to convince you that fresh tuna is superior—it's not! (These were the same people who tried to tell us fresh pasta was better than dried. Remember? They were wrong then, too.) Fresh tuna bears little resemblance to canned, and more often than not, people over-

cook it until it's dry. Fresh tuna is at its best when quickly grilled, or eaten raw as sushi or sashimi, so you won't find any recipes for it in this collection.

Nowadays, nutritionists are touting tuna as health food. Their recent research shows that eating fatty fish like tuna (which contains omega-3 fatty acids) can help guard against macular degeneration and heart attacks and may cut the chances of getting cancer. It's been proven to lower cholesterol and help prevent clogged arteries. It may also reduce the pain of rheumatoid arthritis and help lower high blood pressure, as well as reducing the pain and itching of psoriasis, the symptoms of multiple sclerosis, and the severity of migraine headaches. And, of course, all fish is an excellent source of protein. Tuna is healthful. Tuna is delicious. No wonder we like it so much.

I've had great fun creating this treasury of tuna treats, and I do hope my book will encourage you to expand your repertoire of tried-and-true (or is that old-and-tired?) tuna recipes. I do know that once you feast on some of these fabulous dishes—from the familiar to the fantastic—you'll not only take tuna out of the tin more often, you'll never take tuna for granted again. ◂

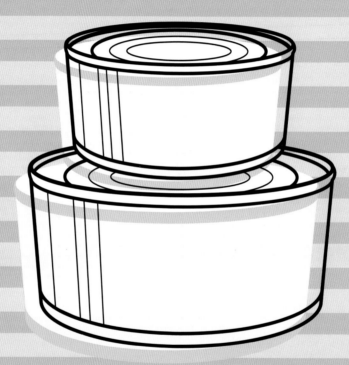

the basics

tuna tips

Tuna connoisseurs know that quality canned tuna is crucial to the success of any recipe. And when tuna is combined with the best ingredients, such as good bread, imported Italian pasta, choice cheeses, top-grade mayonnaise, marinated artichokes, fat black olives, and so on, the results are guaranteed to be totally delicious.

When buying canned tuna, choose tuna packed in olive oil rather than in water for best flavor. Second best is tuna packed in oil, which is usually soy or canola oil (some recipes specify oil-packed or water-packed tuna when the flavor of olive oil would be too strong for the particular dish). If you are counting calories, by all means use water-packed tuna, which has around 36 calories per ounce (drained), whereas oil-packed has 56 calories per ounce (drained), although the final dish won't be nearly as flavorsome.

Tuna is packed in three basic categories: "solid pack" or "fancy," "chunk" or "standard pack," or "flaked." Solid pack consists of large pieces of solid meat with some small fragments. Chunk has three pieces of solid meat with small fragments, and flaked tuna consists entirely of small fragments of meat. The meat in all three categories is of the same quality, so whether it's solid, chunk, or flake doesn't affect the taste, just the price. If you like, use the less-expensive flaked tuna in recipes where it's going to be broken up or mashed into fillings, and solid or chunk tuna in recipes requiring large pieces. I prefer solid pack for my recipes, because I can control the size of the chunks or flakes myself.

Albacore tuna, prized for its white meat, has the mildest flavor. Light-meat tuna comes from yellowfin tuna and sometimes bluefin and skipjack tuna. It is stronger flavored than white-meat tuna. Italians prefer dark-meat tuna, which also comes from the skipjack and is often labeled "tonno." I prefer the rich, meaty taste of tonno or light-meat tuna (packed in olive oil) to white-meat tuna and recommend it in most of my recipes. I know that if you try it, you'll also be very pleased with the results.

Tuna is packed in cans sized $3^{1}/_{4}$ to $3^{1}/_{2}$ ounces, 6 to 7 ounces, $9^{1}/_{4}$ ounces, and $12^{1}/_{2}$ to 13 ounces. The most common can size available in supermarkets is the 6- to 7-ounce size.

The best-quality tuna is tender and has a fresh, clean taste with no fishy aroma. Some brands can taste salty or metallic, or be rubbery or mealy in texture. Try different brands to find the one you like best. Solid light tuna packed in olive oil is very tender, with no fishy flavor, and it adds a depth and richness to many tuna dishes that would otherwise taste bland if water- or oil-packed tuna was used.

An unopened can of tuna will keep for a year on the shelf, if stored in a cool place. Once opened, unused portions of tuna should be transferred to a nonmetal container, covered, and stored in the refrigerator for no more than 3 days.

the tuna pantry

Tinned tuna is one of America's most popular pantry staples, not only because it tastes good, is inexpensive, and is convenient, but because it has the same protein content as eggs, cheese, poultry, and meat. When tuna-friendly pantry items are stocked as well, meal preparation is a snap. Here's a list of ingredients I keep in my kitchen (many of which you may already have) to create an almost limitless variety of quick-to-prepare tuna dishes with terrific flavor at a moment's notice. I haven't listed French, country, and Italian bread or bagels because they are all best on the day they are baked and, unfortunately, don't freeze as well as other breads.

in *the* cupboard

- Anchovies
- Assorted dried pasta
  (extra-wide egg noodles,
  farfalle, fettucine, rigatoni,
  spaghetti, orzo)
- Bottled Thai fish sauce
  (nam pla)
- Bread crumbs
  (dry unflavored)
- Canned artichoke hearts
- Canned black beans
  (frijoles negros)
- Canned chicken broth
  (preferably College Inn brand)
- Canned chickpeas

- Canned tomatoes (not
  packed with added purée)
  (Progresso Tomatoes with Basil)
- Canned water chestnuts
- Canned white kidney beans
  (cannellini)
- Canola oil
- Crackers (preferably
  Carr's Water Crackers)
- Dried cellophane
  (bean thread) noodles
- Dry white vermouth
- Extra-virgin olive oil
- Capers (Goya Spanish Capers)
- Caponata (eggplant appetizer)
- Chili sauce
- Cornichons (sour gherkins)

- Sweet gherkins
- Major Grey's chutney
  (Crosse & Blackwell brand)
- Marinated artichoke hearts
  (Progresso brand)
- Pickled sliced jalapeño
  peppers
- Roasted red peppers
- Medium or hot salsa
- Oyster crackers
- Vinegars (red wine, white
  wine, red balsamic, and
  unseasoned rice wine)
- Rice, long-grain and Arborio
- Tahini (sesame seed paste)
- Tortilla chips

on *the* **counter or in** *a* **basket**

- Baking potatoes

- Garlic

- Onions (red and yellow)

- Tomatoes

from *the* **herb garden**

- Arugula

- Basil

- Chives

- Cilantro

- Dill

- Mint

- Parsley

- Rosemary

- Thyme

in *the* **spice rack**

- Basil

- Bay leaves

- Cayenne pepper

- Curry powder (best quality)

- Oregano

- Red pepper flakes

- Thyme

- Whole black peppercorns
  for the pepper grinder

in *the* **refrigerator**

- Bacon (regular and precooked
  ready-to-use, preferably
  Oscar Mayer brand)

- Bell peppers

- Butter (preferably unsalted)

- Eggs (preferably organic)

- Cheddar cheese (preferably
  well aged, extra-sharp)

- Cream cheese
  (whipped and regular)

- Dijon mustard
  (preferably Maille brand)

- Feta cheese

- Ginger, fresh and crystallized

- Green onions

- Half-and-half

- Heavy cream

- Lemons, limes

- Lettuce

- Milk

- Mayonnaise (preferably
  Hellman's or Best Foods brand)

- Monterey Jack cheese

- Mozzarella cheese
  (low-moisture, whole milk)

- Olives (Kalamata,
  Niçoise, and Gaeta)

- Parmesan cheese
  (freshly grated Parmigiano-
  Reggiano or grana padano)

- Sauerkraut, packaged

- Sour cream

- Sun-dried tomatoes
  (dry or packed in oil)

- Swiss or Gruyère cheese
  (well aged and imported)

in *the* **freezer**

- English muffins

- Flour tortillas

- Lavash (flatbread)

- Pita breads

- Puff pastry

- Vegetables (corn kernels,
  green peas, lima beans)

glossary *of* ingredients

anchovies

Not all anchovies are created equal. The best ones are Italian, come in glass jars, and are reddish brown. The only problem is that the jars contain more anchovies than the more common flat 2-ounce can. Once opened, leftover anchovies can be kept in the refrigerator in the oil for maybe 1 day as they do become fishy. Some canned anchovies are also excellent; try different brands until you find one to your liking.

bacon

I highly recommend Oscar Mayer bacon as the flavor is much superior to other supermarket brands. When testing my recipes, I found some brands had a slightly rancid flavor and left a strange aftertaste.

black olives

Purchase brined olives in bulk from an Italian or Greek market, or look for them in the deli case of some supermarkets. The best olives are Gaeta olives from Italy, Kalamata from Greece, and Niçoise from France. Kalamata olives can be used in any recipe calling for the other brined black olives: they are the most widely available and have the most pungent flavor—which I prefer. Jars of Kalamata olives can now be found in most supermarkets, but not all brands are excellent. The best bottled product I have found is the Peloponnese brand, available both unpitted and pitted. Don't even think of using canned California olives in these recipes. They don't have enough punch. Alert your dinner companions when using unpitted olives.

black pepper

Never use preground black pepper; freshly ground pepper is essential. I like a generous amount of freshly ground black pepper in many of my recipes, as well as an extra dose of pepper at the table. Taste before serving to be sure you've added enough. And don't forget to pass the pepper mill at the table.

bread

Good bread is essential to a great sandwich. I prefer to purchase bread from a quality bakery. Avoid most supermarket baguettes, as they are often fluffy white bread disguised as a French loaf. When I suggest country-style bread, I mean a big, round, white crusty loaf with a nice chewy texture. Good chewy rye or dark pumpernickel bread is also recommended. If unavailable, Pepperidge Farm is a good supermarket brand for both pumpernickel and Jewish rye bread.

butter

I prefer the taste of unsalted (sweet) butter, but if you like salted butter, by all means use it.

capers

The unopened flower buds of a Mediterranean shrub, these are pickled in brine. There are two types, the tiny nonpareil variety and the larger pea-sized ones. Unless otherwise specified, they can be used interchangeably in most recipes; just remember that the larger type has more punch and that is why I prefer them.

TOMATO

CILANTRO

GARLIC

cilantro

Also known as fresh coriander, this pungent herb is usually either loved or hated. I happen to love it, but I always ask my dinner guests first before adding it to a dish. When in doubt, I simply place it in a small serving bowl and allow everyone to add it at the table. Flat-leaf (Italian) parsley or basil can often—but not always—be substituted for cilantro. Do a taste test first to see.

dried herbs

Many cooks don't realize that dried herbs and spices lose color, flavor, and fragrance over time. Replace your shelf stock if you know the herbs are past their prime— they will have lost their bright color and fresh aroma.

feta cheese

A slightly firm, salty white cheese, originally from Greece, feta is available in most supermarkets, specialty cheese shops, and Greek food markets. It adds a delicious salty tang to many dishes.

fresh herbs

Don't substitute dried herbs if fresh is specified in the recipes in this book. Many supermarkets carry fresh basil, flat-leaf (Italian) parsley, rosemary, and cilantro. If yours doesn't, start now to encourage them to do so.

garlic

Never, ever substitute powdered garlic in these recipes. Ditto the minced variety that comes in jars. Always chop garlic fresh, preferably just before adding it to the dish. Not only is the flavor superior, but it has lots of health-giving properties, too. Nowadays, nice plump garlic bulbs are available in most markets. When a recipe calls for a big, fat garlic clove it's the equivalent of about 2 large garlic cloves, but use your own judgment: some cloves are so humongous, they are the equivalent of 3 or even 4 large garlic cloves! Let your taste buds be your guide. My philosophy is, when in doubt, add more!

olive oil

Good-quality extra-virgin olive oil (first cold pressing) is important to many recipes. If you stint on quality, the dish will suffer. When I specify "fruity" olive oil, I mean a greenish-gold, extra-virgin olive oil with a pleasant fruity flavor. Good general-purpose supermarket brands are Bertolli or Colavita.

parmesan cheese

Be sure to purchase Italian Parmesan with the words *Parmigiano-Reggiano* or *grana padano* stamped on the rind. I prefer to buy a big wedge from an Italian deli or grocer and grate it just before using. If you store the wedge in a zippered, heavy plastic freezer bag in the refrigerator, it will keep for 2 to 3 months. Never use the prepackaged brands that are now available in supermarkets (even the "gourmet" brands in plastic containers, labeled to appear authentically Italian), as they taste truly awful. Also avoid the shrink-wrapped wedges found in the cheese section of supermarkets. Some gourmet food shops, Italian delis, and cheese stores pre-grate Parmigiano-Reggiano (it will be labeled as such). If you know it is freshly grated, then—and only then—you have

BLACK OLIVES

ROSEMARY

ANCHOVIES

my permission to use it! Just remember that Parmesan begins to lose flavor soon after grating.

red pepper flakes

Also known as crushed red pepper or hot red pepper flakes, these fiery shards give a flavor boost to many dishes, so don't leave them out. Some brands are hotter than others and they do lose heat over time, so taste and adjust the amounts accordingly.

roasted red peppers

Although homemade roasted peppers taste best, there are many bottled products to choose from on the market today. Different brands vary dramatically in quality. When choosing the bottled product, look for bright red peppers with bits of black char still clinging to them.

salt

Unfortunately, fear of salt has prompted many cooks to abandon it, but without it, your food will taste flat. Unless you're on a salt-restricted diet, make sure you add enough to bring out the flavors of the ingredients. I have given amounts in my recipes, but they are only guides. Taste before adding any salt, then add only as much as tastes right to you.

sun-dried tomatoes

Purchase reddish — not brownish — tomatoes, packed in olive oil, although I usually use the dry-packed tomatoes sold loose in specialty food markets and some supermarkets. I place them in a colander, pour boiling water over to soften, then drain. I then pack them into a clean jar and cover with olive oil and perhaps some fresh basil. They'll be ready to use immediately.

tomatoes

Use only full-flavored, vine-ripened tomatoes. If your tomatoes are flavorless, your food will be, too. To seed, cut them in halves or quarters and use your fingers to remove the seeds, then gently squeeze to remove the juice. There's no need to skin tomatoes unless you feel it's necessary. If full-flavored tomatoes are not available, try substituting plum or cherry tomatoes. They often have more flavor than winter tomatoes.

zest

The colored layer of skin on a citrus fruit adds wonderful flavor to many dishes. Be careful not to remove any of the white pith, which can be bitter.

equipment

Cooking with tuna requires no special tools—except perhaps a good can opener! Kidding aside, the most important thing for any good cook is to use heavy-duty pots and pans. Take a trip to a restaurant supply store for large (12-inch), heavy nonstick skillets, and check kitchen ware shops for good, heavy nonreactive saucepans such as Calphalon. Sharp knives are also a necessity, as are a food processor, a blender, of course, kitchen scissors for snipping herbs, a good citrus zester, a kitchen scale, a pepper mill, and tongs. You probably already have most, if not all, of the above in your kitchen.

CHAPTER TWO

tuna starters, snacks,
and palate teasers

In this chapter, you'll find appealing appetizers and nibbles from all over the world, all of them easy to make and fun to eat. Travel the globe tasting ITALIAN ANTIPASTI, SPANISH TAPAS, and FRENCH AMUSE-GUEULES — everything from classic TUNA TAPENADE to elegant TUNA-EGGPLANT CAPONATA, and all-American faves like TEX-MEX TUNA DIP and CREAM CHEESE AND TUNA PÂTÉ. Served on your best china and accompanied with a glass of wine, these tasty treats are proof positive of just how TOTALLY DELICIOUS, exciting, and (yes!) stylish good old tinned TUNA can be!

tuna tapenade

MAKES ABOUT ³/₄ CUP ●◄

---

1 medium garlic clove

1 small can (about 3 ounces) solid light tuna packed in olive oil, undrained

3 anchovy fillets

1 tablespoon drained capers

¹/₄ cup Kalamata or Niçoise olives, pitted, plus very coarsely diced olives for garnish (optional)

¹/₄ cup mayonnaise

¹/₈ teaspoon cayenne pepper

PREPARATION

From southern France comes this robust sauce— quite similar to Italy's *tonnato* sauce—to spread on French bread, crostini, water crackers, or bagels. Or serve it as a dip with bread sticks or crudités; spoon it over cold poached fish or chicken; or drizzle some over a crunchy salad. Make an easy Niçoise-style potato salad by tossing the tapenade (thinned with a little olive oil) over halved cooked tiny red-skinned potatoes and halved cooked green beans. Garnish the salad with Niçoise or Kalamata olives.

step 1. Chop the garlic in a food processor. Add the tuna with its oil, the anchovies, capers, olives, mayonnaise, and cayenne and whirl just until combined but still chunky.

step 2. Transfer to a bowl, cover, and refrigerate for up to 2 days. Just before serving, garnish the tapenade with diced olives, if desired.

tex-mex tuna dip

MAKES ABOUT 1 CUP

1 can (about 6 ounces) solid or chunk light tuna packed in oil, well drained

1 large green onion, green tops only, chopped

3 tablespoons chopped pickled jalapeño peppers

1/2 cup mayonnaise

1/4 cup fresh cilantro leaves, finely chopped

2 tablespoons fresh lime juice

Salt and freshly ground black pepper

Tortilla chips for serving

This simple dip is easy to make and surprisingly good, but if you're not a cilantro aficionado, don't even think of making it. Cilantro is what gives the dip that extra zip—without it, it's bland and boring. Serve with best-quality tortilla chips and ice-cold Mexican beer or margaritas.

PREPARATION

Combine the tuna, green onions, jalapeños, mayonnaise, cilantro, lime juice, and salt and pepper to taste in a medium serving bowl. Serve with tortilla chips.

cream cheese *and* tuna pâté

MAKES ABOUT 1½ CUPS ➤

1 package (8 ounces) cream cheese, at room temperature

1 can (about 6 ounces) solid light tuna packed in olive oil, well drained

2 to 3 tablespoons fresh lemon juice

6 heaping tablespoons snipped fresh chives, dill, or flat-leaf parsley

Salt and freshly ground black pepper

Crackers or sliced crusty baguette for serving

Cornichons for serving (optional)

Whip up this smooth, spreadable pâté that is perfect with water crackers or crusty French bread, or try it as a spread for tiny tea sandwiches. If you make the pâté ahead of time and refrigerate it, bring it to room temperature before serving. As a substitution for the herbs, stir in ¼ cup chopped green olives or capers. You can also substitute a little of the caper liquid for some of the lemon juice. Serve with imported cornichons. You may substitute plain, soft goat cheese for the cream cheese.

PREPARATION

Whirl the cream cheese, tuna, lemon juice, chives, and salt and pepper to taste together in a food processor until thoroughly combined. Transfer to a serving bowl, place on a platter, and surround with crackers or a sliced crusty baguette. Serve with cornichons, if you like.

VARIATIONS

to *make* **tuna dip fines herbes**

Whirl enough sour cream into the pâté mixture to make it of dunking consistency and stir in a combination of snipped fresh chives, parsley, tarragon, and thyme.

for **tuna horseradish dip**

Blend 1 drained 6-ounce can solid light tuna packed in olive oil with about ½ cup mayonnaise. Stir in some chopped green onion tops and parsley, salt, pepper, cayenne pepper, and prepared horseradish to taste. Serve with grilled or toasted pita triangles.

tuna, lemon, *and* caper crostini

MAKES ABOUT 24 CROSTINI

1 sourdough baguette (about 2 inches in diameter), cut into ½-inch-thick slices

Fruity olive oil for brushing

1 big, fat garlic clove, peeled and left whole

1 can (about 6 ounces) solid light tuna packed in olive oil, undrained

6 anchovy fillets

½ cup fresh flat-leaf parsley

1 tablespoon drained capers, plus extra for garnish

2 tablespoons mayonnaise

Salt and freshly ground black pepper

2 teaspoons fresh lemon juice

About 48 strips roasted red pepper, bottled or homemade (see page 73)

Grated zest of 3 large lemons

Large basil leaves for garnish

Crostini, those wonderful Italian toasts topped with all sorts of savory ingredients, are here highlighted with a pungent purée of parsley, tuna, lemon, capers, and olive oil. To make the final preparation easy, prepare the purée and crostini separately in advance, then simply spread, serve, and enjoy (with a glass of lightly chilled Italian Chardonnay).

PREPARATION

step 1. Preheat the oven to 400° F.

step 2. Brush each slice of bread lightly on both sides with olive oil. Place on a baking sheet and bake for 4 to 5 minutes on each side, until crisp and golden; let cool. (The crostini may be made ahead up to this point and stored in an airtight container for 1 day.)

step 3. Chop the garlic in a food processor. Add the tuna with its oil, the anchovies, parsley, capers, mayonnaise, salt and pepper to taste, and lemon juice and whirl just until combined but not completely smooth. (The purée can be prepared a few hours in advance, covered, and refrigerated until serving.)

step 4. When ready to serve, spread the tuna purée on the crostini, mounding slightly and not spreading all the way to the edge. Garnish with the red pepper strips, capers, and lots of lemon zest. Arrange on a serving tray on top of large basil leaves, if desired. Serve at once.

VARIATIONS

to *make* **italian tuna** *and* **caper spread**

Blend 1 drained 6-ounce can solid light tuna packed in olive oil with 6 anchovies, 2 tablespoons drained capers, ¹/₂ cup (1 stick) unsalted butter at room temperature, 2 teaspoons fresh lemon juice, and salt and pepper to taste in a food processor (not a blender). Just before serving, spread it on crostini, water crackers, or slices of crusty bread. Garnish each one with slivers of red pepper and a couple of capers.

for **french tuna** *and* **brandy pâté**

Make the Italian tuna and caper spread. Chill, then, just before serving, stir in 1 tablespoon brandy. Serve with crackers, crostini, or a sliced crusty baguette.

tuna fondue

MAKES 4 TO 6 SERVINGS ►◄

3 tablespoons unsalted butter

$^1/_2$ cup chopped green onions, including the green tops

$^1/_4$ cup all-purpose flour

$2^1/_2$ cups half-and-half

$^1/_4$ cup medium-dry sherry

2 cups (8 ounces) shredded imported aged Swiss or Gruyère cheese

1 teaspoon salt

1 to 2 teaspoons Tabasco sauce

1 can (about 6 ounces) solid light tuna packed in olive oil, well drained and broken into small pieces

1 to 2 sourdough baguettes, cut into large cubes

Crudités for serving, such as carrot and fennel sticks, broccoli and cauliflower florets

Next time you're snowbound, make this easygoing snack or supper dish to serve in front of the fire. You must use well-aged imported cheese for the best flavor, and because otherwise the fondue might turn grainy rather than smooth and creamy. You will also need a fondue pot and forks, plenty of bread, and, for extra warmth, a bottle of wine.

PREPARATION

Melt the butter in a heavy, medium saucepan over medium-high heat. Add the green onions and cook for several seconds, or until fragrant. Stir in the flour, reduce the heat to medium-low, and cook for 3 minutes, stirring with a wooden spoon. Add the half-and-half and whisk until it just comes to a boil. Reduce the heat and stir in the sherry, cheese, salt, and Tabasco and continue stirring until the cheese is melted and thoroughly combined. Stir in the tuna, then transfer the mixture to a fondue pot over low heat. Adjust the heat so the mixture just barely simmers. Serve with bread cubes and crudités.

hot 'n' cheesy tuna dip *with* garden vegetables

MAKES ABOUT 2¹/₂ CUPS ➥◄

1 tablespoon unsalted butter

1 big, fat garlic clove, minced or put through a garlic press

1 cup half-and-half

1 package (8 ounces) cream cheese, at room temperature, cut into small pieces

1 small can (about 3 ounces) solid light tuna packed in olive oil, well drained and broken into small chunks

1 large tomato (¹/₂ pound), seeded and chopped

¹/₄ cup snipped fresh chives or chopped green onion tops

1 can (4 ounces) diced green chilis, fire roasted

1 teaspoon red Tabasco sauce

1 teaspoon green Tabasco sauce

¹/₄ cup fresh cilantro or flat-leaf parsley, finely chopped

¹/₂ teaspoon salt

Freshly ground black pepper

Crudités for serving: broccoli florets, cauliflower florets, radishes (thinly sliced), thickly julienned bell peppers, fennel, carrots, and so on

Tortilla chips or crusty French bread for serving

This creamy tuna dip contains a hefty jolt of jalapeños and is served hot and bubbly from the oven. It makes a simple snack when served with crispy crudités and crusty French bread for dunking. Make it ahead of time, if you prefer, then pop it in the oven just before serving.

PREPARATION

step 1. Preheat the oven to 375º F.

step 2. Melt the butter in a heavy, medium saucepan over medium-high heat until sizzling. Add the garlic and cook for several seconds, or until fragrant. Add the half-and-half and bring just to a simmer; don't let it boil. Add the cream cheese and whisk until smooth. Remove from the heat and add the tuna, tomato, chives, chilis, red and green Tabasco sauces, cilantro, salt, and pepper to taste. Stir to combine well.

step 3. Pour the mixture into a 1-quart ramekin or soufflé or casserole dish. Bake for 20 minutes, or until hot and bubbly. Serve hot with crudités and tortilla chips or crusty French bread.

deep-fried tuna wontons *with* plum sauce

MAKES ABOUT 50 WONTONS ➤

1 jar (10 ounces) best-quality sweet-and-sour duck sauce (La Choy brand)

1 can (about 6 ounces) solid light tuna packed in oil, well drained

2 ounces cream cheese, at room temperature

3 tablespoons coarsely diced crystallized ginger

1 teaspoon Tabasco sauce

2 tablespoons drained chopped pickled jalapeño peppers

$1/4$ cup snipped fresh chives or chopped green onion tops

6 whole canned water chestnuts, drained and diced

$1/2$ teaspoon salt

Grated zest of 2 large limes

About 50 square wonton wrappers

About 50 fresh cilantro leaves (optional)

Canola oil for deep-frying

Consider making these crispy wontons with their surprise filling of crystallized ginger, cream cheese, and tuna to pass around at your next cocktail party. The cilantro is optional, but it gives the filling that extra oomph.

PREPARATION

step 1. Place the sweet-and-sour duck sauce in a small bowl. Set aside for a dipping sauce.

step 2. Combine the tuna, cream cheese, crystallized ginger, Tabasco sauce, jalapeños, chives, water chestnuts, salt, and lime zest in a medium bowl and stir until thoroughly mixed.

step 3. Place 1 teaspoon of the tuna mixture in the center of each wonton wrapper and top the filling with a large cilantro leaf, if using. Brush a circle of water around the filling. (I dip my finger in a small bowl of water and use it as a "brush.") Pull up the sides, then pinch the wrapper to enclose the filling and form a pouch. Carefully pull out the four corners at the top to form a frill.

step 4. Heat about 1 inch of oil in a heavy saucepan over high heat to 350° F. Fry the wontons in batches for 1 to 2 minutes, or just until lightly golden; do not over-brown. Using a skimmer, transfer the wontons to a paper towel–lined tray to drain. Serve at once, with the dipping sauce.

thai tuna cakes *with* chili dip

MAKES 4 TO 6 SERVINGS ➤◄

chili dip

¹/₄ cup water

¹/₄ cup unseasoned rice vinegar

¹/₄ cup sugar

2 tablespoons Thai fish sauce (nam pla)

1 teaspoon red pepper flakes

1 green onion, including the green tops, chopped

1 medium garlic clove, minced or put through a garlic press

thai tuna cakes

3 tablespoons canola oil, plus more if needed

¹/₄ cup diced red bell pepper

¹/₂ teaspoon red pepper flakes

2 green onions, chopped, white and green parts kept separated

2 big, fat garlic cloves, minced or put through a garlic press

1 tablespoon finely chopped fresh ginger

¹/₄ cup diced green beans

¹/₂ cup fresh cilantro leaves, chopped

Finely grated zest of 2 medium limes

1 tablespoon Thai fish sauce (nam pla)

¹/₄ teaspoon salt

2 cans (about 6 ounces each) solid light tuna packed in olive oil, well drained and broken into small chunks

1 ounce (1 small bundle) cellophane (bean thread) noodles, soaked in hot water for 10 minutes, then drained and snipped into 1-inch pieces

1 large egg, beaten

Scant ¹/₂ cup cornstarch

Tiny Thai-like tuna cakes contain colorful flecks of red pepper, crunchy green beans, green onion, cilantro, and transparent cellophane noodles. Dipped in a tangy sweet and sour sauce, these tasty morsels make a great appetizer. The dip and tuna cakes can be made ahead, covered, and refrigerated, but don't fry them until the last minute.

PREPARATION

step 1. Combine all the chili dip ingredients in a small bowl until the sugar is dissolved. Divide the dip among 4 to 6 small dipping bowls and set aside.

step 2. Heat 1 tablespoon of the oil in a large, heavy, nonstick skillet over medium-high heat. Add the bell pepper, red pepper flakes, the white part of the green onion, the garlic, ginger, and green beans. Cook for 2 minutes, or until the vegetables are crisp-tender.

Transfer to a bowl and let cool. Stir in the cilantro, green onion tops, lime zest, fish sauce, salt, and tuna. Stir in the noodles, egg, and cornstarch until thoroughly combined. Form the mixture into about 24 small meatballs—squeezing gently as they tend to fall apart—and place on a baking sheet. Flatten the balls slightly into patties, cover with plastic wrap, and chill for a minimum of 30 minutes or up to 3 hours before cooking.

step 3. In a large, heavy, nonstick skillet, heat the remaining 2 tablespoons oil over medium-high heat until hot. Cook the patties in batches, for 2 minutes each side, or until heated through and golden brown on both sides, adding more oil as necessary. Using a metal spatula, transfer the patties to a paper towel–lined tray to drain; keep warm in a low oven until all are completed. Divide the tuna cakes among 4 to 6 plates and set the individual bowls of chili dip alongside.

tuna tapas

MAKES ABOUT 12 TAPAS ➤◀

½ loaf sourdough baguette, cut into ½-inch-thick slices (12 slices)

3 to 4 tablespoons fruity olive oil

1 big, fat garlic clove, minced or put through a garlic press

3 to 4 plum tomatoes, thinly sliced crosswise

Salt and freshly ground black pepper

About ¼ cup well-drained solid light tuna packed in olive oil, broken into small pieces

About 4 ounces thinly sliced imported Swiss or Gruyère cheese

Finely chopped fresh cilantro or parsley leaves

Bite-sized tapas are Spanish appetizers served in cafes, bars, and restaurants accompanied by a glass of wine or sherry and good conversation. This traditional tapa of tuna, tomatoes, and cheese-topped croutons is one of the easier ones to make, and it's even easier to eat.

PREPARATION

step 1. Preheat the oven to 400° F. Line a baking sheet with aluminum foil. Arrange the bread slices in one layer on the prepared baking sheet.

step 2. Combine the olive oil and garlic in a small bowl and brush both sides of the bread rounds with the garlic oil. Bake for 4 to 5 minutes each side, or until crisp and golden. Remove from the oven (leave the oven on) and top each bread slice with a tomato slice; sprinkle with salt and pepper to taste. Place a little tuna on each, then top with a slice of cheese (the same size as the bread round) and a generous sprinkling of cilantro. Sprinkle with salt and pepper again.

step 3. Return to the oven and heat for 4 minutes or just until the cheese is melted. Serve hot.

tuna plate *with* cilantro salsa, olives, *and* roasted red peppers

MAKES 2 SERVINGS ●◄

2 big, fat garlic cloves

¼ cup pickled sliced jalapeño peppers

1½ pounds (about 3 large) tomatoes, quartered and seeded

¼ teaspoon salt

½ cup fresh cilantro leaves, chopped

1 tablespoon fruity olive oil

1 tablespoon fresh lime juice

A handful of mesclun (mixed baby salad greens)

2 cans (about 3 or 6 ounces each) solid light tuna packed in olive oil, well drained

¼ cup roasted red peppers, bottled or homemade (see page 73), cut into thick julienne

A handful of green or pimiento-stuffed green olives

A handful of Kalamata or mixed black olives

Tortilla chips or French bread for serving

Not your typical lunch-plate special, this vibrant starter, salad, or snack can be put together with minimal effort. To make it easier still, substitute best-quality store-bought salsa and freshen it up with cilantro, chilis, and lime juice, if necessary. Offer a basket of tortilla chips or thick slices of French bread on the side.

PREPARATION

step 1. Coarsely chop the garlic in a food processor, or by hand. Add the jalapeños and tomatoes and coarsely chop—do not purée. Transfer the mixture to a medium bowl and stir in the salt, cilantro, and olive oil. Add the lime juice. Set aside.

step 2. Decorate 2 dinner plates with the salad greens and invert a small or regular-sized can of tuna in the center of each one. Top the tuna with salsa to taste. Surround the tuna with the roasted red peppers and green and black olives. Serve with tortilla chips or French bread and extra salsa on the side.

VARIATIONS

to *make* italian antipasto plate

Arrange some or all of the following ingredients in rows over a large platter: Two drained 6-ounce cans of solid light tuna packed in olive oil, 1 can drained anchovies (rolled or flat), marinated artichoke hearts, roasted red peppers, Kalamata olives, slices of Italian cured meats such as salami and/or prosciutto, and Gorgonzola cheese or sliced fresh mozzarella cheese. Serve with a loaf of crusty Italian or French bread.

tuna-eggplant caponata

MAKES ABOUT 1 CUP ◄

1 can (about 6 ounces) solid light tuna packed in olive oil, well drained

1 can (about 7½ ounces) caponata

Sliced French bread, crostini, or water crackers for serving

Caponata is a classic antipasto consisting of eggplant, celery, capers, olives, and onions in a sweet-and-sour tomato sauce. The canned variety is very convenient and a pantry staple in my kitchen. It's also very versatile, and I often mix it with a tin of tuna to serve as an appetizer or snack spread on sliced crusty French bread, water crackers, or crostini. It's also delicious as a tuna salad on lettuce or as a sandwich filling between lengthwise slices of crusty French bread. It's good, too, tossed over steaming hot spaghetti, along with some diced fresh tomatoes, fresh basil, butter, and Parmesan cheese. You can spread it over a homemade pizza crust, then top it with fresh tomato slices and mozzarella cheese. Canned caponata can be found in the supermarket section with marinated artichokes, roasted red peppers, and the like.

PREPARATION

Combine the tuna and caponata in a small bowl. Serve with French bread, crostini, or water crackers.

tuna-anchovy puffs

MAKES ABOUT 24 TUNA PUFFS

1 small can (about 3 ounces) solid light tuna packed in olive oil, well drained

1 can (2 ounces) anchovy fillets, drained and chopped

$1/4$ cup mayonnaise

$1/8$ teaspoon cayenne pepper

2 tablespoons freshly grated Parmesan cheese

One 2-sheet package (about 1 pound) frozen puff pastry, thawed

1 large egg beaten with 1 tablespoon water

Coarsely ground black pepper for garnish (optional)

Lure your cocktail party guests to the hors d'oeuvres tray with these cute little cut-out puff-pastry "fishes" filled with tasty tuna, anchovies, and Parmesan cheese. The "fishes" make a perfect conversation starter, but for ease of preparation, feel free to simply cut the pastry into small squares. I like to serve the tuna puffs as a "school of fish" nestled in baby curly-leaf lettuce (the waves) on a sea-blue platter (see photo, page 2).

PREPARATION

step 1. Preheat the oven to 375° F.

step 2. Mash the tuna with the anchovies, mayonnaise, cayenne, and Parmesan cheese in a small bowl until well combined.

step 3. Lay 1 sheet of puff pastry flat on a lightly floured work surface and roll it out to a 14-by-15-inch rectangle.

step 4. Repeat with the other pastry sheet.

step 5. Brush off the excess flour and spread the tuna mixture over one of the pastry sheets. Cover with the second pastry sheet and use a rolling pin to gently press the sheets together.

step 6. Cut out the pastry using a 3- to 4-inch fish-shaped pastry or cookie cutter, or cut it into squares using a pizza cutter or pastry wheel.

step 7. Arrange the pastry fish or squares on a lightly greased baking sheet. Brush the tops lightly with some of the egg mixture. Make fish "eyes" with a small piece of black pepper, if desired. Bake for 8 to 10 minutes, or until puffed and golden; don't overbrown or the pastry will be bitter. Transfer to a serving platter and serve hot.

tuna-*and*-bacon-stuffed baked potatoes

MAKES 4 TO 8 SERVINGS ◅

4 large baking potatoes
(about 12 ounces each)

$1/4$ cup ($1/2$ stick) unsalted butter,
at room temperature

$3/4$ cup sour cream

$1/2$ cup coarsely chopped fresh
chives or chopped green onion tops

1 teaspoon salt

Freshly ground black pepper

$1/8$ teaspoon cayenne pepper, plus
extra for garnish

4 crisp-cooked bacon slices (Oscar
Mayer brand), very coarsely diced

1 can (about 6 ounces) solid light
tuna packed in olive oil, well drained
and broken into large chunks

Melted butter for brushing

You don't have to be a kid to enjoy these comforting spuds, a savory mixture of mashed potatoes, sour cream, chives, tuna, and bacon bits stuffed and baked in a potato skin until nice and crusty on top. They make a very hearty snack, luncheon dish, or casual supper with a salad on the side. This recipe doesn't require bacon fat, so it's quick and convenient to use packaged precooked bacon, and the bonus is there's no greasy pan to clean.

PREPARATION

step 1. Preheat the oven to 425° F. Line a baking sheet with aluminum foil.

step 2. Bake the potatoes for 1 hour or until tender. Remove from the oven, let cool to the touch, then cut in half lengthwise. Carefully scoop out most of the potato flesh from each half, leaving $1/4$-inch-thick shells. Mash the hot potato flesh with the butter and sour cream in a medium bowl. Gently stir in the chives, salt, pepper to taste, cayenne, bacon, and tuna. Spoon the mixture back into the potato skins and brush the tops with a little melted butter. Sprinkle with cayenne pepper, if desired.

step 3. Place the stuffed potatoes on the prepared baking sheet and bake for 15 minutes, or until heated through and crusty on top. Let the potatoes cool slightly before serving. Pass the pepper mill.

tuna soups *and* chowders

This collection of recipes features simple, SUSTAINING SOUPS and CHUNKY CHOWDERS, some ideal for chilly evenings, others perfect for a light lunch or a quick supper. TUNA soups are easy and economical, and most of the following recipes can be made in minutes with staples from the pantry. Furthermore, many of the soups are meals in themselves. So all you need to prepare a delicious bowlful is to turn on the stove, maybe sauté a few vegetables, add a splash or two of cream, toss in a sprinkling of thyme, a tin of TUNA, some frozen corn—and *voilà*! You've got a SENSATIONAL SOUP that rivals even the best clam chowder!

tuna *and* sweet corn chowder

MAKES 6 TO 8 SERVINGS ➤◄

6 bacon slices (Oscar Mayer brand), cut crosswise into ½-inch pieces

1 big, fat garlic clove, chopped

2 medium onions, chopped

2 tablespoons all-purpose flour

4 cups homemade chicken stock or canned broth

8 ounces boiling potatoes, peeled and cut into ½-inch dice

½ bay leaf

½ teaspoon dried thyme

½ teaspoon salt

Freshly ground black pepper

1 cup heavy cream

3 cups fresh or frozen corn kernels

1 cup frozen baby lima beans (optional)

1 can (about 6 ounces) solid light tuna packed in olive oil, well drained and broken into large chunks

Chopped fresh flat-leaf parsley or thyme sprigs for garnish

When the nights get a little nippy, I often make this comforting meal-in-a-bowl. It's my take on clam chowder using tuna instead of clams, and I might add, it's just as delicious. To make the soup even more substantial, add a cup of frozen baby lima beans along with the corn. Sprinkle the steaming bowls of soup with fresh parsley or thyme, and serve with hot biscuits or oyster crackers. Serve a refreshing fruit salad for dessert to make a perfectly balanced meal.

PREPARATION

step 1. Cook the bacon until crisp in a large, heavy saucepan over medium-high heat. Pour off all but 1 tablespoon of the bacon fat. Add the garlic and onions and cook for 1 minute, or until tender. Stir in the flour, reduce the heat to medium-low, and cook, stirring constantly with a wooden spoon, for 3 minutes.

step 2. Add the chicken stock, potatoes, bay leaf, thyme, salt, and pepper to taste and bring the soup just to a boil. Immediately reduce the heat and gently simmer for 15 minutes, or until the potatoes are thoroughly tender.

step 3. Stir in the heavy cream, corn, lima beans (if using), and tuna and cook until heated through. Ladle into soup bowls and garnish with parsley or sprigs of thyme. Serve hot.

tuscan tuna, bean, *and* tomato soup

MAKES 6 TO 8 SERVINGS ➤

2 tablespoons fruity olive oil, plus extra for serving

3 big, fat garlic cloves, chopped

1 medium onion, chopped

1 scant tablespoon fresh rosemary leaves, finely chopped

1 teaspoon dried oregano

$^1/_2$ teaspoon red pepper flakes

1 can (28 ounces) tomatoes (not packed with added purée), undrained and puréed in a blender

2 cans (16 ounces each) white kidney beans (cannellini), undrained and puréed in a blender

2 cans (about 6 ounces each) solid light tuna packed in olive oil, well drained and broken into flakes with some small chunks

1 teaspoon salt

Freshly ground black pepper

Chopped fresh flat-leaf parsley for garnish

PREPARATION

I hope the Tuscans will forgive me, but I think tuna adds another dimension to their wonderful soup. It mingles marvelously with the smooth cannellini-bean-thickened soup, adding depth of flavor and richness. Herb focaccia, grilled slices of Italian bread, or a crusty baguette and, perhaps, a salad of bitter greens are all that's needed for a filling, satisfying supper. Use a blender, not a food processor, to purée the beans and tomatoes.

step 1. Heat the olive oil in a large, heavy, nonreactive saucepan over high heat. Add the garlic and onion and cook for 2 minutes, or until they just begin to turn golden. Add the rosemary, oregano, and red pepper flakes and stir for a few seconds to release their aroma. Stir in the puréed tomatoes, puréed beans, tuna, salt, and pepper to taste.

step 2. Bring the soup to a simmer and cook for 1 minute, or until heated through. Ladle into shallow soup bowls, sprinkle with parsley, and serve hot. Serve with a bottle of olive oil for each person to drizzle over their soup to taste.

broccoli, cheddar, *and* tuna chowder

MAKES ABOUT 6 SERVINGS ➤◄

2 tablespoons unsalted butter

1 big, fat garlic clove, chopped

1 medium onion, chopped

$1/8$ teaspoon cayenne pepper

2 tablespoons all-purpose flour

4 cups homemade chicken stock or canned broth

1 bunch broccoli (about $1^1/2$ pounds), cut into large bite-sized florets (stems discarded or saved for another use)

1 cup (4 ounces) shredded extra-sharp Cheddar cheese, plus extra for garnish

1 cup heavy cream

1 can (about 6 ounces) solid light tuna packed in olive oil, well drained and broken into large chunks

$1/2$ teaspoon salt

Freshly ground black pepper

Chock-full of nourishing broccoli, tuna, and Cheddar, this scrumptious fish chowder makes a marvelous homespun supper when accompanied with a basket of hot-from-the-oven buttermilk biscuits.

PREPARATION

step 1. Melt the butter in a large, heavy saucepan over high heat until sizzling. Add the garlic and onion and cook for 1 minute, or until tender. Add the cayenne and flour, reduce the heat to medium, and cook, stirring constantly with a wooden spoon, for 3 minutes. Add the chicken stock and bring it to a boil over high heat, whisking fairly constantly. Reduce the heat to medium, add the broccoli florets, and gently simmer for 4 to 5 minutes, or just until tender. Reduce the heat to low.

step 2. Add the cheese, a little at a time, to the soup, and stir until melted. Stir in the heavy cream, tuna, salt, and pepper to taste. Increase the heat to medium and cook for 1 minute, or until hot, but do not let it boil. Ladle into soup bowls, sprinkle with a little shredded Cheddar cheese, and serve hot.

quick tuna bisque

MAKES 4 SERVINGS ►◄

2 cups heavy cream

2 cups milk

2 cans (about 6 ounces each) solid light tuna packed in olive oil, drained (but not too well) and broken into small chunks

$1/2$ teaspoon salt

Freshly ground black pepper

$1/4$ teaspoon cayenne pepper

$1/4$ cup coarsely snipped fresh chives or chopped green onion tops

PREPARATION

Don't be fooled by the simplicity of this recipe and "plainness" of the ingredients. This soothing soup takes literally seconds to prepare and offers superior flavor. Don't substitute tuna packed in canola oil, vegetable oil, or water for tuna packed in olive oil. The olive oil adds flavor to the chowder, making it unnecessary to add the typical pat of butter to the soup bowl. Serve the bisque with oyster crackers, saltines, or hot-from-the-oven buttermilk biscuits. Do not substitute half-and-half for the heavy cream and milk.

Heat the cream, milk, tuna (some remaining oil will float on the surface of the soup, adding flavor), salt, pepper to taste, and cayenne in a heavy, medium saucepan over medium-high heat just until hot; don't let the soup boil. Sprinkle with the chives. Ladle into soup bowls and serve hot.

manhattan tuna chowder

MAKES 6 TO 8 SERVINGS ✦◄

8 bacon slices (Oscar Mayer brand), cut crosswise into ¹/₂-inch pieces

1 medium onion, chopped

1 celery stalk, finely chopped

1 carrot, finely chopped

2 big, fat garlic cloves, chopped

¹/₄ teaspoon red pepper flakes

1 can (28 ounces) tomatoes (not packed with added purée), undrained and puréed in a blender

¹/₂ cup roasted red peppers, bottled or homemade (see page 73), coarsely chopped

2 cups homemade chicken stock or canned broth

8 ounces boiling potatoes, peeled and cut into ¹/₂-inch dice

1¹/₂ teaspoons dried oregano

¹/₂ teaspoon dried thyme

¹/₂ teaspoon salt

Freshly ground black pepper

1 can (about 6 ounces) solid light tuna packed in olive oil, well drained and broken into large chunks

Chopped fresh cilantro or flat-leaf parsley for garnish

PREPARATION

I've fashioned this full-bodied and spicy tomato-based soup for lovers of "red" clam chowder, who, I'm pretty positive, will find this tunafish variation equally tasty. What I found while creating the recipes for this book was how often tinned tuna doesn't taste like tinned tuna—more like a mild-tasting generic fish, which is good, since it makes canned tuna extremely versatile. You could call this recipe "Manhattan fish chowder" and your dinner companions would probably never guess what kind of fish it was. They would just think it delicious. Oyster crackers, garlic toasts, or chewy bread goes great on the side and, if you're serving this as a simple soup supper, serve a tossed green salad alongside, if you like. This soup is best served freshly made as it thickens quite a bit on standing.

step 1. Cook the bacon until beginning to crisp in a large, heavy, nonreactive saucepan over medium-high heat. Remove all but 1 tablespoon of the bacon fat. Add the onion, celery, carrot, and garlic and cook for 4 minutes, or until tender. Add the red pepper flakes, tomatoes, roasted red peppers, chicken stock, potatoes, oregano, thyme, salt, and pepper to taste and bring the soup just to a boil over high heat.

step 2. Reduce the heat and gently simmer for 15 minutes, or until the potatoes are thoroughly tender. Stir in the tuna and simmer until heated through. Ladle into soup bowls and garnish with cilantro or parsley. Serve hot.

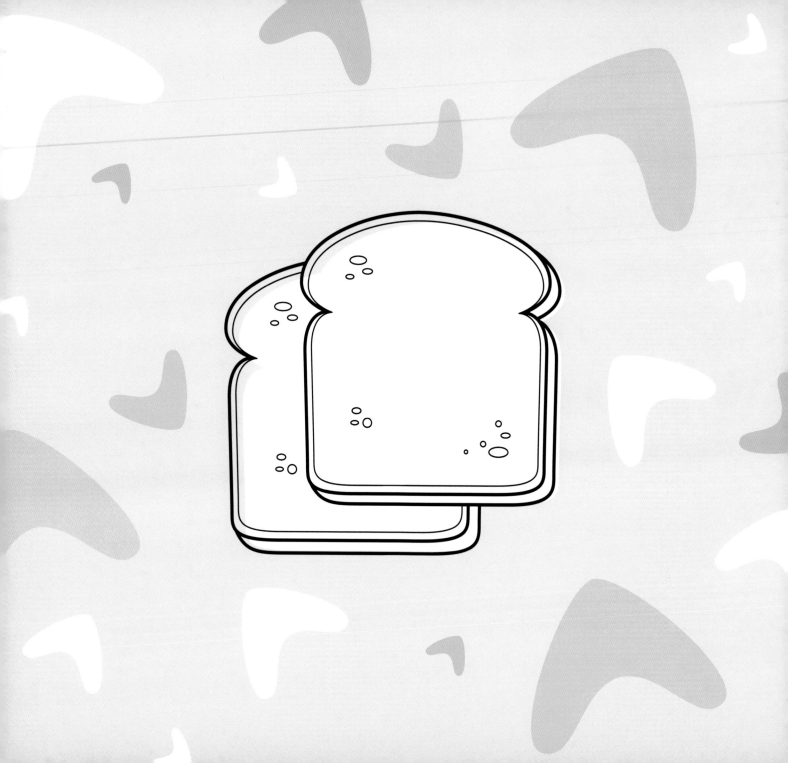

tuna sandwiches

Because you can never have too many good TUNA sandwich recipes, I've created a collection of sixteen fabulous fillings featuring fresh and exciting additions like roasted red peppers, black olives, and arugula that are guaranteed to make TUNA-sandwich lovers rejoice. Some of the sandwiches, such as NOT-YOUR-MOTHER'S TUNA MELT and CLASSIC TUNA SALAD SANDWICH, are casual, some more sophisticated, and all are the essence of simplicity. Whether the fillings are nestled between slices of rustic country bread or focaccia, stuffed into pita rounds, or tucked inside a tortilla roll, these bountiful handfuls will have you wondering why you've been eating plain old ordinary TUNA salad sandwiches all these years.

tuna niçoise sandwich

MAKES 4 SANDWICHES ◄◄

A handful of mesclun (mixed baby salad greens)

Four 5-inch lengths crusty baguette, halved lengthwise

1 can (about 6 ounces) solid light tuna packed in olive oil, well drained and broken into large chunks

2 big, fat garlic cloves, minced or put through a garlic press

6 anchovy fillets, very coarsely chopped

2 tablespoons drained capers

3 tablespoons fruity olive oil

2 tablespoons fresh lemon juice

2 hard-cooked eggs, peeled and sliced crosswise

1 jar (about 6 ounces) marinated artichoke hearts, very well drained and sliced

12 oil-packed sun-dried tomato halves, drained

1/4 cup Niçoise or Kalamata olives, pitted and halved

You'll definitely say goodbye to your old, ordinary tuna sandwiches after you try the compelling flavors and textures of the famous salade Niçoise tucked inside a crusty French baguette.

PREPARATION

step 1. Arrange the salad greens over the bottom halves of the bread.

step 2. Gently stir together the tuna, garlic, anchovies, capers, olive oil, and lemon juice in a medium bowl and divide the mixture among the sandwich bottoms. Top with the egg slices, artichoke hearts, sun-dried tomatoes, and olives. Cover with the top halves, then carefully press down on the sandwiches to compress the ingredients. Serve at once.

classic tuna salad sandwich

MAKES 4 LARGE SANDWICHES ⬤‹

2 cans (about 6 ounces each) solid light tuna packed in olive oil, well drained and broken into large chunks

$^1/_2$ cup mayonnaise

1 tablespoon fresh lemon juice

1 cup very coarsely chopped Granny Smith apple (unpeeled)

$^1/_2$ cup finely chopped celery heart (no leaves)

$^1/_2$ cup finely diced red onion

$^1/_4$ teaspoon salt

Freshly ground black pepper

Several leaves fresh watercress, arugula, or curly-leaf lettuce

8 slices pumpernickel or rye bread

Is there anyone who doesn't know how to make the classic, all-American tuna sandwich? In case there are a few out there who don't, here it is, with a few pointers. It is preferable to use good pumpernickel or rye bread, but even white bread is forgiven here, and French bread or whole wheat is good, too. Instead of iceberg lettuce, line the bread slices with peppery watercress or arugula to add a nice bite. For a crunchy tuna salad, I like to add chopped celery heart, tart apple, or cucumber, or all three (about 1$^1/_2$ cups total) and another $^1/_2$ cup diced red onion. Or, you can simply add chopped celery heart to the tuna mixture and top the sandwich with thinly sliced cucumbers and/or red onions if you like. Some people like to add a layer of sliced dill pickle or gherkins or add a sprinkling of capers or chopped green or black olives to the tuna mixture (omitting the apple, of course); the more daring like diced anchovies. As with many tuna sandwich fillings, this is delicious served sans bread as a salad atop shredded lettuce; or simply serve it as a spread (chopping the ingredients into slightly smaller pieces) on thick slices of French bread or crackers.

PREPARATION

step 1. Combine the tuna, mayonnaise, lemon juice, apple, celery, onion, salt, and pepper to taste in a medium bowl until well mixed but not mushy.

step 2. Arrange the greens over 4 of the bread slices. Divide the tuna salad over the greens and top with the remaining bread. Cut into halves and serve.

VARIATION

to *make* **a classic american tuna melt**

Preheat the broiler. Top slices of lightly toasted pumpernickel or rye bread with the tuna salad. Top with shredded Monterey Jack, Cheddar, Swiss, or fontina cheese and broil for a few minutes, or until the cheese is melted and the filling is hot.

pan bagna

MAKES 1 SANDWICH ◄

1 crusty round roll, about 5 inches in diameter	A few slices marinated artichoke hearts	Soft white goat cheese, at room temperature
A small handful of watercress or lettuce leaves	A few pitted, sliced black olives (Niçoise or Kalamata)	2 tablespoons fruity olive oil
2 slices large, ripe tomato	Several capers	1 tablespoon red wine vinegar
A few chunks of olive oil–packed tuna, well drained	1 small garlic clove, finely chopped	Chopped fresh basil
1 thin crosswise slice red bell pepper, raw or roasted	A few thin slices red onion	Dried thyme
	4 anchovy fillets	Salt and freshly ground black pepper

PREPARATION

The French call this robust salad-in-a-sandwich *pan bagna*, which means "bathed bread." I like to serve these at casual summer gatherings. Simply set out the ingredients and make them to order. You must have good-quality round, crusty sandwich rolls or lengthwise bread slices from a large baguette. Soft, fluffy bread or rolls just won't do. The following toppings are for one sandwich; just increase the amounts according to the number of servings required.

step 1. Cut the roll in half lengthwise and pull out some of the inside of the bread halves, leaving a 1/2-inch shell.

step 2. Place the watercress, tomato, tuna, bell pepper, artichokes, olives, capers, garlic, onion, and anchovies on the bottom half of the roll. Spread the top half of the roll with goat cheese and set aside. Whisk the oil, vinegar, basil, and thyme together in a small bowl. Drizzle the dressing over the filling, then sprinkle with salt and pepper to taste. Top the sandwich with the remaining roll half. Traditionally, the top is placed on and pressed down, then the whole thing is wrapped tightly and enjoyed several hours later, after the flavors have melded. Provide plenty of napkins.

pita pockets *stuffed with* curried tuna salad

MAKES 4 TO 8 SANDWICHES ►◄

2 cans (about 6 ounces each) solid light tuna packed in olive oil, well drained and broken into large chunks

$1/4$ cup drained sliced pickled jalapeño peppers, chopped

$1/2$ cup mayonnaise

1 tablespoon fresh lime juice

2 teaspoons best-quality curry powder

$1/4$ cup diced celery heart

$1/4$ cup diced red onion

$1/2$ cup dark raisins

$1/2$ cup very coarsely chopped Granny Smith apple (unpeeled)

$1/4$ cup fresh basil leaves, chopped

Salt

Several lettuce leaves, shredded

2 to 4 pita pocket breads, warmed and halved crosswise

PREPARATION

Tuna is terrific mixed with curry-flavored mayonnaise, tiny bits of celery heart, and sprightly green basil. I've also added dark raisins and diced green apples for more crunch and sweetness. The Curried Tuna and Chutney Salad with Mango (page 89) also makes an interesting tuna sandwich filling. This filling is also delicious between pumpernickel or 5-inch lengthwise slices (about 6) of a crusty baguette.

step 1. Gently combine the tuna, jalapeños, mayonnaise, lime juice, curry powder, celery heart, red onion, raisins, apple, basil, and salt to taste in a medium bowl.

step 2. Stuff some shredded lettuce into the pita halves and divide the filling among the 4 to 8 pita pockets. Serve at once.

not-your-mother's tuna melt

MAKES 6 OPEN-FACED SANDWICHES ►◄

3 English muffins, split in half

Tuna and Artichoke Heart Salad (facing page), at room temperature

1 1/2 cups (6 ounces) shredded Swiss, Gruyère, Monterey Jack, mozzarella, or extra-sharp white Cheddar cheese

6 Kalamata olives, pitted and halved

Capers for garnish

A Mediterranean twist on the classic American tuna melt is made with an artichoke heart salad mixture mounded on toasted English muffins, topped with imported Swiss cheese, Kalamata olives, and capers, then broiled until hot and bubbly. Serve with cherry tomatoes and nippy arugula lightly drizzled with balsamic vinegar and fruity olive oil.

PREPARATION

step 1. Preheat the broiler.

step 2. Line a baking sheet with aluminum foil and place the muffin halves, cut side up, on the foil. Place under the broiler about 4 inches from the heat source for 1 to 2 minutes, or until the tops are lightly toasted. Remove from the oven (leave the broiler on) and divide the tuna salad among the toasted muffin halves, piling it on generously. Top with the shredded cheese, 2 olive halves each, and several capers.

step 3. Broil for 2 to 3 minutes, or until the cheese is bubbling and lightly speckled with brown. Turn off the broiler and let the sandwiches stay in the oven for about 1 minute to heat the filling through. Remove the sandwiches and serve at once.

tuna *and* artichoke heart salad sandwich

MAKES 4 SANDWICHES ◂◄

2 cans (about 6 ounces each) solid light tuna packed in olive oil, well drained and broken into small chunks

2 teaspoons fresh lemon juice

1 teaspoon dried oregano

Salt and freshly ground black pepper

1 jar (6$^{1}/_{2}$ ounces) marinated artichoke hearts, drained and coarsely chopped

$^{1}/_{2}$ cup mayonnaise

Several lettuce leaves

4 crusty sandwich rolls, halved lengthwise

PREPARATION

I like to stuff pita pockets with this appetizing salad or serve it simply as a spread with a sliced baguette. It's also delicious in crusty buns or on toasted and buttered thin rye bread—or even good old white bread. Try it as a summer salad in hollowed-out tomatoes or stuffed in cherry tomatoes as an hors d'oeuvre.

step 1. Gently stir the tuna, lemon juice, oregano, salt and pepper to taste, artichokes, and mayonnaise together in a medium bowl until combined.

step 2. Arrange the lettuce on the bottom halves of the rolls. Divide the salad among the sandwich bottoms and top with the remaining rolls.

hawaiian tuna melt

MAKES 6 OPEN-FACED SANDWICHES 🐟

1 can (about 6 ounces) solid light tuna packed in olive oil, well drained and broken into large chunks

1/4 cup mayonnaise

2 teaspoons fresh lemon juice

1/4 cup coarsely snipped fresh chives

2 tablespoons chopped fresh flat-leaf parsley

Salt and freshly ground black pepper

3 English muffins, split in half

6 canned pineapple slices, patted dry

About 1/2 cup alfalfa sprouts (optional)

6 crisp-cooked bacon slices (Oscar Mayer brand), halved crosswise

6 ounces shredded Monterey Jack cheese or mozzarella (1 1/2 cups)

This succulent hot sandwich will appeal to fans of bacon, cheese, and pineapple pizzas. *Aloha!*

PREPARATION

step 1. Combine the tuna, mayonnaise, lemon juice, chives, parsley, and salt and pepper to taste in a bowl.

step 2. Preheat the broiler.

step 3. Line a baking sheet with aluminum foil and place the muffin halves, cut side up, on the foil. Place under the broiler, about 4 inches from the heat source, for 1 to 2 minutes, or until the tops are lightly toasted. Remove from the oven (leave the broiler on) and divide the tuna mixture among the muffin halves. Top each with a pineapple slice, some alfalfa sprouts, if using, 2 bacon pieces, and some of the cheese.

step 4. Broil for 2 to 3 minutes, or until the cheese is bubbling and lightly speckled with brown. Turn off the broiler and let the sandwiches stay in the oven for about 1 minute to heat the filling through. Remove from the oven and serve at once.

pesto tuna sandwich

MAKES 4 LARGE SANDWICHES ►◄

¹/₄ cup plus 2 tablespoons homemade or store-bought pesto sauce

¹/₄ cup mayonnaise

2 cans (about 6 ounces each) solid light tuna packed in olive oil, well drained and broken into large chunks

2 ripe, medium tomatoes, seeded and coarsely chopped

Salt and freshly ground black pepper

Shredded lettuce

8 slices pumpernickel or crusty white country-style bread or 4 warmed pita pocket breads, halved crosswise

PREPARATION

Being a big pesto fan, I paired the potent sauce with mayonnaise, tuna, and tomatoes to make a piquant sandwich filling that's perfect to stuff between slices of chewy pumpernickel, country bread, or into a warm pita pocket. Instead of fresh tomatoes, use sun-dried tomatoes. Throw in a few halved, pitted Kalamata olives, too, if you like. This is also delicious served as a spread.

step 1. Combine the pesto, mayonnaise, tuna, tomatoes, and salt and pepper to taste in a medium bowl.

step 2. Arrange shredded lettuce on 4 of the bread slices or stuff some shredded lettuce in each pita half. Divide the filling among the slices or pitas. Top with the remaining bread slices, if using, and cut the sandwiches in half. Serve at once.

tuna caesar salad sandwich

MAKES 4 TO 6 SANDWICHES ✇

Four to six 5-inch lengths crusty baguette, halved lengthwise

Fruity olive oil for drizzling, plus 1/4 cup

1 big, fat garlic clove, minced or put through a garlic press

8 anchovy fillets, coarsely chopped

3 tablespoons fresh lemon juice

1 teaspoon whole-grain or Dijon mustard

1/2 teaspoon Worcestershire sauce

2 tablespoons freshly grated Parmesan cheese

4 cups very coarsely chopped romaine lettuce hearts

1 can (about 6 ounces) solid light tuna packed in olive oil, well drained and broken into large chunks

Salt and freshly ground black pepper

I've never met anyone who doesn't like Caesar salad. And I love it so much, I even wrote a whole book on the subject. I combined the zestily dressed greens with everything from blue cheese to smoked salmon to deep-fried oysters, but never tinned tuna—until now. So here's my mini tuna Caesar to toss and enjoy in crusty lengths of toasted French bread—the bread, of course, being the stand-in for the croutons. Hail Caesar!

PREPARATION

step 1. Preheat the broiler.

step 2. Drizzle each cut side of the bread with olive oil and place the pieces, cut side up, on a baking sheet.

Place them under the broiler, about 4 inches from the heat source, for 30 seconds to 1 minute, or just until lightly toasted; watch carefully so they don't overbrown.

step 3. Whisk the garlic, anchovies, 1/4 cup olive oil, lemon juice, mustard, and Worcestershire sauce together in a medium bowl until blended. Add the Parmesan cheese, lettuce, tuna, and salt and pepper to taste and gently toss to mix.

step 4. Divide the mixture among the bottom halves of the bread and cover with the top halves. Serve at once. Provide plenty of napkins.

tuna reuben sandwich

MAKES 4 SANDWICHES ━◄

1 can (about 6 ounces) solid light
tuna packed in olive oil, well drained
and broken into large chunks

2 tablespoons mayonnaise

1 tablespoon bottled chili sauce
or ketchup

1 big, fat garlic clove, minced
or put through a garlic press

$^1/_4$ cup diced red onion

2 tablespoons prepared hot
horseradish, drained

$^1/_4$ teaspoon salt

8 slices Jewish rye
or pumpernickel bread

Room-temperature butter for
spreading

Dijon mustard for spreading

1 cup sauerkraut, well drained

8 ounces shredded imported
Swiss or Gruyère cheese

Reuben sandwiches are named after the famous New York delicatessen Reuben's. Typically made with rye bread, they are piled high with thin slices of corned beef, fresh sauerkraut, and Swiss cheese, then fried on the griddle until the cheese melts through the filling and into the toasty bread. I couldn't resist the idea of replacing the corned beef with tuna, and the resulting flavor was anything but boring. Serve these sandwiches with deli-style dill pickles on the side, if you wish.

PREPARATION

step 1. Combine the tuna, mayonnaise, chili sauce, garlic, red onion, horseradish, and salt in a medium bowl.

step 2. On a large piece of wax paper, generously spread one side of each bread slice with butter. Turn the slices over and place on wax paper, buttered side down. Spread the other side of the bread slices with Dijon mustard. Divide the tuna mixture among 4 of the bread slices and top with sauerkraut and shredded cheese. Top with the remaining bread slices, buttered side up. Carefully press down on the sandwiches to compress the ingredients.

step 3. Cook the sandwiches for about 3 minutes on each side in 1 or 2 large nonstick skillets over medium-high heat, pressing down on them with a spatula, until the tuna is heated through, the cheese is melted, and the bread is golden brown. Cut the sandwiches in half and serve hot.

tuna, cream cheese, *and* caper wraps

MAKES 4 SANDWICHES ➤◀

4 flour tortillas (8 or 9 inches in diameter)

$^1/_2$ cup (4 ounces) whipped cream cheese spread

$^1/_4$ cup drained capers

Salt and freshly ground black pepper

$^1/_4$ cup coarsely snipped fresh chives or chopped green onion tops

Several large fresh basil leaves

1 can (about 6 ounces) solid light tuna packed in olive oil, well drained and broken into large chunks

$^1/_2$ cup coarsely diced peeled cucumber

$^1/_4$ cup diced red onion

$^1/_4$ cup coarsely chopped roasted red pepper, bottled or homemade (see page 73)

Halved lemon for squeezing over filling

No sandwich collection would be complete without this ravishing roll-up. As the saying goes, it's a wrap!

PREPARATION

step 1. Preheat the oven to 250° F.

step 2. Wrap the tortillas in aluminum foil and warm in the oven for 10 minutes.

step 3. To assemble the wraps: Lay the warmed tortillas on the counter. Spread the cream cheese evenly over each one, leaving a 1-inch border all around. Sprinkle the capers, salt, pepper, and chives evenly over the cream cheese. Top with the basil leaves, tuna, cucumber, red onion, and roasted red pepper, distributing them evenly among the tortillas. Sprinkle with a little more salt and pepper and a generous squeeze of lemon juice.

step 4. Fold the bottom of the tortilla halfway up over the filling; then, starting at one end of the unfolded sides, roll the tortilla tightly until it completely encloses the filling, leaving the top open. Place seam side down on a plate and serve.

tuna sandwich *with* roasted red peppers *and* olives

MAKES 2 SANDWICHES ➤

¹/₄ cup coarsely chopped roasted red peppers, bottled or homemade (see page 73)

¹/₄ cup very coarsely chopped Kalamata olives

¹/₄ cup diced celery heart

¹/₄ cup diced red onion

1 can (about 6 ounces) solid light tuna packed in olive oil, well drained and broken into large chunks

¹/₄ cup mayonnaise

Salt and freshly ground black pepper

Several arugula leaves

2 crusty sandwich rolls, halved lengthwise

PREPARATION

People really relish this ultimate tuna sandwich with its tender bits of tuna, ravishing roasted red peppers, dark olives, crunchy onions, and celery. This filling is equally delicious as a salad on a bed of peppery arugula, served with thick slices of French bread on the side. Make sure to use a crusty bread for this beguiling sandwich.

step 1. Combine the red peppers, olives, celery, red onion, tuna, and mayonnaise in a medium bowl. Season to taste with salt and pepper.

step 2. Arrange the arugula leaves on the bottom halves of the rolls. Divide the filling between the sandwiches and top with the remaining roll halves.

bagel, cream cheese, *and* tuna sandwich

MAKES 4 LARGE SANDWICHES

4 large bagels (5 inches in diameter), halved lengthwise

1 cup (8 ounces) whipped cream cheese spread

Coarsely chopped fresh dill for sprinkling

Snipped fresh chives for sprinkling

Several curly-leaf lettuce leaves

1 can (about 6 ounces) solid light tuna packed in olive oil, well drained and broken into large chunks

Halved lemon for squeezing over tuna

Several thin slices red onion

Several thin slices large ripe tomato

Salt and freshly ground black pepper

PREPARATION

When funds are low and lox is too expensive, a frugal tin of tuna will come to the rescue. Begin with bagel halves, then spread with whipped cream cheese sprinkled with fresh herbs, and top with tuna, red onion, tomato, and lettuce for an irresistible contrast of tastes and textures.

Spread all the bagel halves with cream cheese. Sprinkle each half with the dill and chives. Top 4 of the halves with lettuce leaves, tuna chunks, a generous squeeze of lemon juice, the red onion slices, and tomato slices. Sprinkle with salt and pepper to taste. Cover with the remaining bagel halves. Provide plenty of napkins.

tuna-tomato melt

MAKES 4 LARGE OPEN-FACED SANDWICHES ◄●

4 slices crusty white country-style or sourdough bread

Fruity olive oil for brushing

2 to 3 flavorful medium tomatoes, thickly sliced

2 big, fat garlic cloves, minced or put through a garlic press

Salt and freshly ground black pepper

12 large fresh basil leaves

1 can (about 6 ounces) solid light tuna packed in olive oil, well drained and broken into large chunks

1 1/2 cups (6 ounces) shredded provolone cheese

PREPARATION

Here's a tuna melt that's easy to make and sure to be a winner, as long as you use only sweet, fruity tomatoes and crusty, dense bread. For an American tuna-tomato melt, substitute good white bread for the country style; omit the olive oil; spread each toasted bread slice with a half-and-half mixture of mayonnaise and Dijon mustard; top with the tomato, garlic, basil, and tuna; and use extra-sharp white Cheddar in place of the provolone. To turn the tuna melt into crostini, use small rounds of bread that have been brushed with olive oil and lightly toasted in the oven. Top the toast rounds with sliced plum tomatoes and the other ingredients, then serve the tuna crostini as tasty appetizers.

step 1. Preheat the broiler.

step 2. Line a baking sheet with aluminum foil and place the bread on the foil. Brush the olive oil on both sides of the bread. Place under the broiler about 4 inches from the heat source and broil for 30 seconds to 1 minute on each side, or until lightly toasted. Remove from the oven (leave the broiler on) and place the tomato slices on each bread slice. Sprinkle with the garlic; season to taste with salt and pepper. Top each toast with 3 basil leaves, one-fourth of the tuna chunks, and one-fourth of the shredded cheese.

step 3. Broil for 1 to 2 minutes, or just until the tuna is heated through and the cheese is melted; don't overcook. Remove the sandwiches and serve at once.

tuna muffuletta

MAKES 4 TO 6 LARGE SANDWICHES ⬤◄

2 big, fat garlic cloves, minced or put through a garlic press

$^3/_4$ cup Kalamata olives, pitted and very coarsely chopped

$^3/_4$ cup pimiento-stuffed green olives, very coarsely chopped

2 tablespoons drained capers

2 tablespoons finely chopped fresh flat-leaf parsley

2 tablespoons finely chopped fresh basil leaves

$^1/_2$ teaspoon dried oregano

$^1/_4$ cup fruity olive oil

2 tablespoons red wine vinegar

1 crusty baguette, about 3 inches in diameter, halved lengthwise

1 can (about 6 ounces) solid light tuna packed in olive oil, well drained and broken into large chunks

Salt and freshly ground black pepper

Halved lemon for squeezing over filling

About 4 ounces shredded provolone cheese

Invented at the New Orleans Central Grocery, the muffuletta is a big, scrumptious sandwich made of a crusty round loaf filled with a tangy Italian olive salad, cured meats like salami, and sliced cheeses. Here, I've created a marvelous tuna muffuletta made with a crusty baguette. You can add some chopped marinated artichokes and hot pickled peppers, if you like. Though not imperative, making the olive and caper salad several hours ahead or overnight allows the flavors to mingle before using.

PREPARATION

step 1. Combine the garlic, black and green olives, capers, parsley, basil, oregano, olive oil, and red wine vinegar in a medium bowl.

step 2. Pull out some of the inside of the bread, leaving a $^1/_2$-inch shell. Arrange the tuna chunks over the bottom half of the bread, season to taste with salt and pepper, and top with the olive mixture, including all the liquid, and a generous squeeze of lemon juice. Sprinkle with the provolone and cover with the top half of the bread. Wrap the sandwich tightly in aluminum foil. Weight the sandwich with a heavy skillet filled with canned goods and let sit at room temperature for 2 to 4 hours to compress the filling.

step 3. To serve, remove the weights and foil and cut the sandwich into 4 to 6 portions.

grilled eggplant, tuna, *and* roasted red pepper panini

MAKES 8 LARGE SANDWICHES ➤

1 unpeeled medium eggplant, cut crosswise into 1/2-inch-thick slices

Fruity olive oil for brushing and drizzling

1 Tuscan flat round loaf, such as focaccia or ciabatta, about 12 inches in diameter, halved lengthwise

Several lettuce leaves

1 can (about 6 ounces) solid light tuna packed in olive oil, well drained and broken into large chunks

Halved lemon for squeezing over filling

Salt and freshly ground black pepper

4 ounces fresh mozzarella, thinly sliced, or crumbled feta or goat cheese

1 cup thickly julienned roasted red pepper, bottled or homemade (see note)

2 big, fat garlic cloves, minced or put through a garlic press

1 large ripe tomato, thinly sliced

A handful of pitted Kalamata olives

8 large fresh basil leaves, coarsely chopped

Panini means "sandwich" in Italian and "delicious" in any language. **This luscious sandwich is a large, round crusty loaf—either focaccia or ciabatta—layered with grilled eggplant, tuna, fresh mozzarella, roasted red peppers, tomato, black olives, and basil leaves. Homemade roasted red peppers taste best in this sandwich, but you can substitute best-quality bottled if you like. As a variation, replace the eggplant with several quartered marinated artichoke hearts. Sandwiches don't get much better than this.**

PREPARATION

step 1. Preheat the grill or broiler. Brush both sides of the eggplant slices with olive oil. Grill or broil the eggplant slices for 4 minutes on each side, or just until cooked through.

step 2. If the bread is quite thick, pull out some of the inside of the bread but not all of it, leaving a 1/2-inch shell. Drizzle the inside of the bread halves with olive oil. Arrange the lettuce leaves on the bottom half. Top with the tuna, a generous squeeze of lemon juice, a drizzle of olive oil, and a little salt and pepper. Layer the remaining ingredients on top of the tuna, drizzling a little olive oil and lemon juice over each layer and sprinkling each layer with salt and pepper. Top with the remaining bread half. Gently press down on the sandwich to compress the ingredients, and cut it into eight wedges.

note. To roast red peppers, place each pepper over a gas burner or under a preheated broiler, and cook, turning frequently with tongs, until slightly softened and charred in several places. Transfer to a plate, cover with an inverted bowl and, when cool enough to handle, peel and seed the peppers.

CHAPTER FIVE

tuna salads

Here's a selection of spirited salads starring TUNA, vegetables, and fruits to serve as side dishes and main courses, or for lunch out on the patio. Try the famous French SALADE NIÇOISE, a generous platter of TUNA chunks, boiled new potatoes, crisp green beans, quartered hard-boiled eggs, sliced red onion, and tomato rings, all dressed up with a tangy vinaigrette and the TUNA-friendly trio of olives, capers, and lemons. Add French bread and a rosé and any day will turn out sunny! Or consider CURRIED TUNA AND CHUTNEY SALAD WITH MANGO, or LEMONY TUNA SALAD WITH TAHINI DRESSING. The recipes in this chapter are all designed to delight the palate and provide plenty of flavorful, simple tuna salads for you to enjoy all year long.

salade niçoise

MAKES 6 TO 8 SERVINGS ➤◄

niçoise vinaigrette

2 big, fat garlic cloves, minced
or put through a garlic press

2 tablespoons Dijon mustard

1/2 cup fresh lemon juice

1 teaspoon salt

Freshly ground black pepper

1 cup fruity olive oil

salade niçoise

1 pound small red-skinned potatoes,
boiled until tender and halved

1 pound green beans, trimmed and
boiled until crisp-tender

1 can (14 ounces) artichoke hearts,
drained, squeezed dry to remove
excess moisture, and halved

1 cup small cherry tomatoes, left whole

1 can (about 6 ounces) solid light
tuna packed in olive oil, well drained
and broken into large chunks

3 hard-cooked eggs, peeled and
quartered

12 anchovy fillets

1/4 cup drained capers

1 medium-small red onion, very
thinly sliced

1/2 cup Niçoise or Kalamata olives,
pitted or unpitted

1/2 cup chopped mixed fresh herbs:
tarragon, chives, flat-leaf parsley,
and basil

Salt and freshly ground black pepper

Lemon wedges for serving

A feast for the eye as well as the palate, this inter-nationally renowned salad is perfect for outdoor entertaining. For the best flavor, make the salad ahead: arrange the ingredients on a platter, cover with plastic wrap, and refrigerate until serving time. I like to toss the still-warm potatoes and green beans with some of the dressing to allow the hot vegeta-bles to soak up lots of flavor. As with most tuna sal-ads, this one makes a wonderful meal in itself, and it loves the company of a chewy baguette and a lightly chilled rosé.

PREPARATION

step 1. To make the vinaigrette: Whisk the garlic, mus-tard, lemon juice, salt, and pepper to taste in a large bowl. Drizzle in the olive oil while whisking until slightly thickened.

step 2. Gently stir the still-hot potatoes and green beans with about 1/2 cup of the dressing in a large bowl until the vegetables absorb most of the dressing. Attractively arrange the potatoes and green beans, the artichokes, cherry tomatoes, tuna chunks, eggs, anchovy fillets, and capers on a very large platter. Scatter the onion slices and olives over the salad. Drizzle with the remaining dressing to taste. Serve immediately, or cover and refrigerate for several hours. Just before serving, sprin-kle with the herbs and salt and pepper to taste, and gar-nish the platter with the lemon wedges.

lemony tuna salad *with* tahini dressing

MAKES 4 SERVINGS ➤

1/3 cup well-stirred tahini
(sesame paste)

1/3 cup water

Grated zest of 2 medium lemons,
plus extra for garnish

1/4 cup plus 1 tablespoon fresh
lemon juice

1 big, fat garlic clove, minced or
put through a garlic press

1/4 teaspoon salt

Freshly ground black pepper

Several curly-leaf lettuce leaves,
shredded

4 cans (about 3 or 6 ounces
each) solid light tuna packed in
olive oil, well drained

Fresh flat-leaf parsley for garnish

Lemon wedges for serving

Warmed lavash (flatbread)
or grilled or toasted quartered pita
breads for serving

A hearty and unusual Middle Eastern–inspired salad featuring lettuce topped with tuna and a lemony tahini dressing. Serve with warm lavash (Middle Eastern flatbread) or grilled pita pockets, or tuck the lettuce and salad inside the warmed bread and serve as a sandwich. This salad loves lots of lemon and freshly cracked pepper, so don't forget to pass the lemon wedges and the pepper mill. Tahini is available in most supermarkets and natural foods stores.

PREPARATION

step 1. Vigorously whisk the tahini and water together in a medium bowl until combined. Add the lemon zest, lemon juice, garlic, salt, and pepper to taste and continue whisking until smooth. Taste and adjust the lemon juice, if necessary; the dressing should be quite tangy.

step 2. Generously line 4 dinner plates with shredded lettuce. Invert a small or regular-sized can of tuna onto the middle of each plate. Spoon the tahini dressing (be generous) over the tuna, then drizzle a little over the lettuce. Sprinkle with parsley and lemon zest. Serve with lemon wedges on the side and pass the pepper mill and remaining tahini dressing. Serve with warm lavash or pita bread.

spicy mexican tuna, black bean, *and* tomato salad

MAKES 4 TO 6 SERVINGS ➤◄

1¹/₂ cups canned black beans (frijoles negros), rinsed and well drained

1 pound ripe tomatoes, seeded and very coarsely diced

1 can (about 6 ounces) solid light tuna packed in olive oil, well drained and broken into large chunks

1 cup fresh or frozen corn kernels

Grated zest of 1 large lime

2 tablespoons fresh lime juice

¹/₃ cup fruity olive oil

1 big, fat garlic clove, minced or put through a garlic press

1 teaspoon red Tabasco sauce

1 teaspoon green Tabasco sauce

1 teaspoon dried oregano

1 teaspoon ground cumin

¹/₂ teaspoon salt

2 green onions, including green tops, chopped

¹/₄ cup fresh cilantro leaves, chopped

1 cup (4 ounces) crumbled feta cheese

2 Hass avocados, peeled, pitted, and cut into thin wedges, for garnish

Tortilla chips for serving

Mexican inspired, this entrée or side-dish salad is lavished with lime juice and lime zest and pepped up with plenty of Tabasco. The colorful mixture of black beans, tomatoes, tuna, corn kernels, green onions, and snippets of cilantro is topped with crumbled feta cheese and served with thin wedges of avocado. (Don't forget to brush the avocado slices with a little lime or lemon juice to prevent discoloration.) Serve tortilla chips on the side.

PREPARATION

Gently combine the black beans, tomatoes, tuna, corn kernels, lime zest, lime juice, olive oil, garlic, red and green Tabasco sauces, oregano, cumin, salt, green onions, and cilantro in a large bowl. Taste and adjust the seasoning, if necessary. Sprinkle with the feta cheese. Serve at room temperature, garnished with the wedges of avocado. Accompany with tortilla chips.

chickpea *and* tuna salad

MAKES 4 TO 6 SERVINGS ➤◄

1 can (19 ounces) chickpeas, drained

1 big, fat garlic clove, minced or put through a garlic press

1 cup grape tomatoes, halved if large

Grated zest of 1 medium lemon, plus extra for garnish

$1/4$ cup fresh lemon juice

$1/4$ cup fruity olive oil

1 can (about 6 ounces) solid light tuna packed in olive oil, well drained and broken into large chunks

2 large green onions, including green tops, chopped

$1/2$ teaspoon salt

Freshly ground black pepper

$1/2$ cup fresh flat-leaf parsley, coarsely chopped

Similar to Tuscan Tuna, Celery, and White Bean Salad (facing page), this earthy salad matches meaty chickpeas and tuna with tiny grape tomatoes in an extra-lemony olive oil dressing. Serve on a bed of arugula, garnish with lots of lemon zest, and accompany with crusty bread. If grape tomatoes are unavailable, substitute halved or quartered cherry tomatoes.

PREPARATION

Gently stir the chickpeas, garlic, tomatoes, lemon zest, lemon juice, olive oil, tuna, green onions, salt, and pepper to taste together in a medium bowl until combined. Just before serving, stir in the parsley. Serve at room temperature, garnished with lemon zest.

tuscan tuna, celery, *and* white bean salad

MAKES 4 SERVINGS ➤◄

1 can (about 6 ounces) solid light tuna packed in olive oil, well drained and broken into large chunks

1 can (19 ounces) white kidney beans (cannellini), rinsed and drained

1 big, fat garlic clove, minced or put through a garlic press

$^1/_4$ cup diced celery heart

$^1/_4$ cup diced red onion

$^1/_4$ cup drained capers

Grated zest of 1 medium lemon

$^1/_4$ cup fresh lemon juice

$^1/_4$ cup fruity olive oil

$^1/_4$ teaspoon red pepper flakes

1 tablespoon Dijon mustard

$^1/_2$ teaspoon salt

Freshly ground black pepper

$^1/_4$ cup fresh flat-leaf parsley, coarsely chopped

Large fresh basil leaves for garnish

Very coarsely diced tomatoes for garnish

PREPARATION

Like most Italian tuna salads, this one is simple and delightful to serve on a sunny terrace. I like to spoon the salad in the center of white dinner plates and circle the salad with large basil leaves and diced tomato (see photo, page 7). Serve with good country bread, and a glass of wine.

Gently stir the tuna, beans, garlic, celery, red onion, capers, lemon zest, lemon juice, olive oil, red pepper flakes, mustard, salt, and pepper to taste in a medium bowl until combined. Just before serving, stir in the parsley. Garnish each plate by surrounding the salad with basil leaves and tomatoes.

tuna coleslaw *with* grapes

MAKES 4 SERVINGS ❖

Mixed baby salad greens (mesclun)

1 can (about 6 ounces) solid or chunk light tuna packed in oil, well drained and broken into large chunks

1^1/$_2$ cups red and green seedless grapes, halved crosswise, plus small grape clusters for garnish

^{1}/$_4$ cup diced red onion

^{1}/$_4$ cup diced celery heart

Grated zest of 2 limes, plus extra for garnish

1 teaspoon fresh lime juice

^{1}/$_4$ teaspoon salt

Freshly ground black pepper

3 tablespoons mayonnaise

2 tablespoons sour cream

1 cup combination of shredded mixed broccoli stems, carrots, and red cabbage

Juicy red and green grapes, julienned vegetables, and bits of tuna tossed in a sour-cream dressing make a wonderfully crunchy, sweet-tasting salad. Spoon the salad over baby greens and garnish each plate with small clusters of grapes. For convenience, you may use the prepared broccoli slaw available in plastic bags from the supermarket in the salad section. It should contain shredded broccoli stems, purple cabbage, and carrots. If broccoli slaw is unavailable, substitute the classic coleslaw mix: cabbage, carrots, and red cabbage.

PREPARATION

step 1. Line 4 dinner plates with the salad greens.

step 2. Gently combine the tuna, grapes, red onion, celery, lime zest, lime juice, salt, pepper to taste, mayonnaise, sour cream, and shredded vegetables together in a medium bowl. Divide the mixture among the plates on top of the greens. Garnish the plates with the grape clusters, sprinkle each salad with lime zest, and serve.

italian rice salad *with* tuna, tomatoes, *and* artichokes

MAKES 6 TO 8 SERVINGS

1^1/$_2$ cups water

1 cup long-grain rice

1 teaspoon salt

1 can (about 6 ounces) solid light tuna packed in olive oil, well drained and broken into large chunks

2 ripe, medium tomatoes, very coarsely diced

^{1}/$_4$ cup diced red onion

1 jar (6 ounces) marinated artichoke hearts, well drained and very coarsely chopped

3 tablespoons drained capers

3 tablespoons finely chopped fresh flat-leaf parsley

1 red bell pepper, roasted, peeled, and very coarsely diced (see page 73)

^{1}/$_2$ cup Kalamata olives, pitted and halved

^{1}/$_3$ cup fruity olive oil

2 tablespoons red wine vinegar

Freshly ground black pepper

Here, tuna enjoys the company of its frequent friends—tomatoes, artichokes, roasted red peppers, and Kalamata olives. Don't make this fresh-tasting salad too far ahead, since it is best served at room temperature. But if pressed, you can cook the rice a few hours ahead of time, cover, and refrigerate it. Bring it back to room temperature before tossing with the remaining ingredients. Let the salad stand for 1 hour so the rice can absorb all of the flavors.

PREPARATION

step 1. Bring the water to a boil in a heavy, medium saucepan over high heat. Stir in the rice and ^{1}/$_2$ teaspoon salt. Reduce the heat to medium-low, cover, and cook for 20 minutes, or until the liquid is absorbed and the rice is tender. Transfer the rice to a large bowl and let cool to room temperature.

step 2. Add the tuna, tomatoes, red onion, artichoke hearts, capers, parsley, roasted red pepper, and olives to the rice and gently stir just until combined.

step 3. Whisk the oil, vinegar, ^{1}/$_2$ teaspoon salt, and pepper to taste together in a small bowl and pour over the rice. Gently stir to combine. Let stand at room temperature for 1 hour before serving. Taste and adjust the seasoning, if necessary. Serve at room temperature.

orzo salad *with* tuna, artichokes, *and* roasted red pepper

MAKES 4 TO 6 SERVINGS ➤◄

1 cup orzo (rice-shaped pasta)

3 tablespoons fruity olive oil

Grated zest of 1 medium lemon

3 tablespoons fresh lemon juice

2 teaspoons Dijon mustard

1 can (14 ounces) artichoke hearts, well drained and squeezed to remove excess liquid, then cut into thirds

1 can (about 6 ounces) solid light tuna packed in olive oil, well drained and broken into large chunks

2 large green onions, including green tops, chopped

1 red bell pepper, roasted, peeled, and very coarsely chopped (see page 73)

2 tablespoons drained capers

½ teaspoon salt

Freshly ground black pepper

¼ cup fresh basil leaves, chopped

2 tablespoons chopped fresh flat-leaf parsley

PREPARATION

Orzo pasta, teamed with tangy artichokes, briny capers, and roasted red pepper, and accented with lemon, fresh parsley, and basil, is another tantalizing variation on the tuna salad theme. This salad is easily portable to take to a potluck picnic or buffet. Or, for an attractive presentation, serve the salad in hollowed-out large tomatoes.

step 1. Cook the orzo in a medium saucepan of boiling salted water until al dente.

step 2. Meanwhile, whisk the olive oil, lemon zest, lemon juice, and mustard together in a large bowl. Drain the orzo and add it to the bowl with the dressing. Gently stir in the artichoke hearts, tuna, green onions, roasted red pepper, capers, salt, and pepper to taste. Let cool to room temperature. Just before serving, stir in the basil and parsley. Serve at room temperature or chilled.

tunisian tuna salad *with* oven-grilled vegetables

MAKES 4 TO 6 SERVINGS ⬣◄

4 big, fat garlic cloves, coarsely chopped

1 large red bell pepper, seeded, deribbed, and cut into 1-by-$^1/_2$-inch pieces

1 large yellow bell pepper, seeded, deribbed, and cut into 1-by-$^1/_2$-inch pieces

2 unpeeled Japanese eggplants, cut into $^1/_2$-inch-thick rounds

1 medium red onion, cut into 1-inch chunks

$^1/_3$ cup fruity olive oil

1 pound ripe plum tomatoes, quartered and seeded

1 can (about 6 ounces) solid light tuna packed in olive oil, well drained and broken into large chunks

$^1/_2$ teaspoon salt

Freshly ground black pepper

2 tablespoons fresh lemon juice

$^1/_2$ cup fresh mint leaves, coarsely chopped

$^1/_2$ cup fresh flat-leaf parsley, chopped

$^1/_2$ cup Kalamata olives, left whole or pitted and halved

$^1/_4$ cup drained capers

Lemon wedges for serving

A variety of vegetables are oven-grilled for a slight smoky flavor, then tossed with tuna, refreshing mint, parsley, black olives, and capers. Somewhat reminiscent of French ratatouille and Italian caponata, this delightful salad is terrific accompanied with grilled pita wedges or crusty bread (or tuck the salad inside the bread for a wonderful sandwich); or serve it as a pasta sauce by tossing the room-temperature tuna mixture with hot rigatoni (adding a little more olive oil, if necessary).

PREPARATION

step 1. Preheat the oven to 450° F. Line a large, heavy baking sheet with aluminum foil.

step 2. Combine the garlic, red and yellow peppers, eggplants, and red onion in a large bowl. Stir in the olive oil. Spread the vegetables in a single layer on the prepared baking sheet (do this in batches if necessary). Roast for 20 to 30 minutes, or until the vegetables are tender and their edges are lightly charred. Transfer to a large bowl.

step 3. Preheat the broiler. Place the tomatoes on the same baking sheet and broil 3 inches from the heat source for 5 minutes, or until they dry out somewhat and are lightly charred on the edges. Transfer to the bowl with the other vegetables.

step 4. Gently stir in the tuna, salt, pepper to taste, lemon juice, mint, parsley, olives, and capers. Serve with lemon wedges.

tuna tabbouleh *with* feta cheese

MAKES 4 TO 6 SERVINGS ➤◄

1 cup bulgur wheat

2 cups boiling water

8 ounces cherry tomatoes, halved

2 large green onions, including green tops, chopped

$^1/_2$ cup fresh flat-leaf parsley, chopped

$^1/_4$ cup fresh mint leaves, chopped, plus mint sprigs and extra leaves for garnish

$^1/_4$ cup fresh lemon juice

$^1/_4$ cup fruity olive oil

1 can (about 6 ounces) solid light tuna packed in olive oil, well drained and broken into large chunks

$^1/_2$ teaspoon salt

Freshly ground black pepper

About 10 Kalamata olives, unpitted or pitted

1 cup (4 ounces) crumbled feta cheese

Refreshingly seasoned with lots of lemon, fresh mint, and parsley, this piquant salad of bulgur and tomato features pungent Kalamata olives, chunks of tuna, and tangy feta cheese. Grilled pita bread is the perfect accompaniment. This is another great summer salad to serve for an outdoor lunch.

PREPARATION

step 1. Combine the bulgur and boiling water in a large heatproof bowl. Let stand for 30 minutes, or until tender but still chewy. Drain in a fine-mesh sieve, gently squeezing out any excess water with the back of a spoon.

step 2. Empty the bulgur into a large bowl. Add the tomatoes, green onions, parsley, mint, lemon juice, olive oil, tuna, salt, and pepper to taste and gently toss to mix. Cover and refrigerate for several hours, if desired.

step 3. To serve, spoon the salad into a mound on a large dinner plate or round platter. Arrange the olives and mint sprigs around the edge and sprinkle the top with feta cheese and mint leaves.

curried tuna *and* chutney salad *with* mango

MAKES 4 SERVINGS ►◄

¹/₄ cup mayonnaise

¹/₄ cup bottled Major Grey's chutney, any large pieces coarsely chopped

2 teaspoons best-quality curry powder

1 tablespoon fresh lime juice

¹/₄ teaspoon salt

2 cans (about 6 ounces each) solid light tuna packed in olive oil, well drained and broken into large chunks

¹/₄ cup diced red onion

¹/₄ cup diced celery heart

¹/₄ cup fresh basil leaves, chopped

2 ripe but firm mangoes, peeled, cut from the pit, and cubed

Several curly-leaf lettuce leaves, shredded

Snipped fresh chives for garnish

PREPARATION

Here's another scrumptious luncheon salad to serve outdoors on the patio. Or try this sweet combination as a sandwich filling for a warmed pita pocket with lots of shredded lettuce, or between toasted slices of pumpernickel or rye bread.

step 1. Combine the mayonnaise, chutney, curry powder, lime juice, and salt in a medium bowl.

step 2. Add the tuna, red onion, celery, and basil and stir just to blend. Gently stir in the mangoes. Cover and refrigerate for at least 2 hours before serving.

step 3. To serve, arrange the shredded lettuce leaves over 4 dinner plates, then divide the salad over the lettuce, arranging it attractively in a high pile in the center of each plate. Sprinkle the salad with chives.

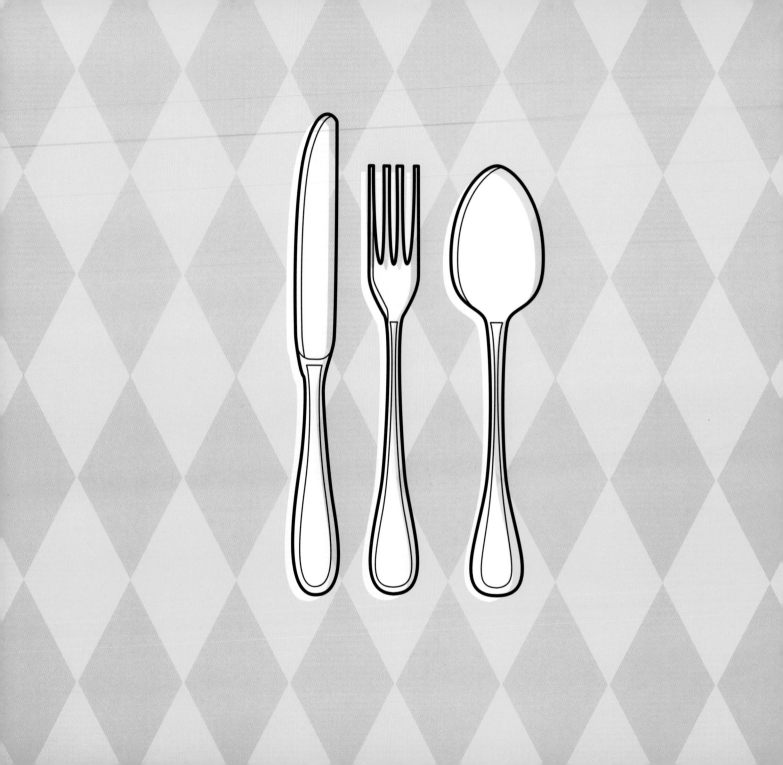

elegant *and* **easy entrées** *for* **breakfast, brunch, lunch,** *or* **supper**

The truth is, a lot of TUNA-based meals have gotten a bad rap—mostly because of those TUNA-casserole concoctions from the fifties, made with canned mushroom soup and mushy, overcooked macaroni. While the recipes in this section include many of those old, comforting family favorites, there's a real difference here: these are classy, sophisticated dishes with an emphasis on fresh ingredients. You'll also find an amazing range of specialties—mostly from the Mediterranean—that includes terrific ITALIAN PASTAS and RISOTTOS tossed with tantalizing TUNA sauces; fabulous tuna-topped pizzas; and savory rice and egg dishes with a surprising array of ingredients. Other classics and variations on the theme are TUNA STROGANOFF, EGGPLANT AND TUNA GRATIN, TUNA TETRAZZINI, PORTUGUESE RICE AND TUNA CASSEROLE, and TUNA AND ROSEMARY PIE, to name a few. So turn the page and treat yourself to the tempting tuna treats that follow.

terrine *of* tuna *and* potatoes

MAKES 6 SERVINGS ➤◄

5 large baking potatoes (about 3 pounds), peeled and cubed

2 cans (about 6 ounces each) solid light tuna packed in olive oil, drained (reserve the oil) and broken into large chunks

1¼ teaspoons salt

Freshly ground black pepper

About 1 cup mayonnaise

1 large red bell pepper, roasted, peeled, and very coarsely chopped (see page 73)

1 jar (3 ounces) capers, drained

Finely chopped fresh flat-leaf parsley for garnish

Cornichons for serving

Niçoise or Kalamata olives for serving

Crusty bread for serving

A simple and delicious French preparation, this terrine makes a great luncheon dish. Make it the centerpiece on a colorful ceramic platter, and don't forget to put out lots of crusty bread and the tuna-friendly trio of capers, cornichons, and olives.

PREPARATION

step 1. Cook the potatoes in an extra-large saucepan of boiling salted water for 8 minutes, or until completely tender but not mushy. Drain and mash the potatoes, then beat in the reserved tuna oil, salt, and pepper to taste.

step 2. Mash the tuna with a fork in a large bowl until fairly smooth. Stir in the mashed potato mixture, mayonnaise, and roasted red pepper until thoroughly combined. (The mixture may need a little more mayonnaise for a smooth texture.) Transfer to a 1½-quart porcelain terrine or soufflé dish. Cover with plastic wrap and refrigerate for at least 2 hours.

step 3. Just before serving, decorate the top of the terrine with some of the capers and the parsley. Accompany with the remaining capers, the cornichons, olives, and bread.

tuna *and* rosemary pie

MAKES 6 TO 8 SERVINGS ◄

1/4 cup (1/2 stick) unsalted butter

2 medium onions, chopped

1/4 cup all-purpose flour

1 can (about 6 ounces) chunk light tuna packed in water, drained (reserve the liquid), and broken into large chunks

About 3/4 cup milk

4 large baking potatoes (about 3 pounds), peeled and cubed

1 big, fat garlic clove, peeled and left whole

1 tablespoon fresh rosemary leaves, finely chopped

1/2 cup snipped fresh chives or chopped green onion tops

1 teaspoon salt

1/2 teaspoon coarsely ground black pepper

Pastry for single-crust pie, homemade or store-bought

1 tablespoon milk for brushing

Mashed potatoes and canned tuna baked in a pie may sound a little unusual, but this adaptation of a French-Canadian classic makes very fine cold-weather eating. Green peas are usually added to the mashed potato mixture, but I've replaced them with a little chopped rosemary instead. Feel free to stir in some frozen tiny peas, if you like, but I prefer to serve them, or another green vegetable, on the side.

PREPARATION

step 1. Melt the butter in a heavy, medium saucepan over medium-high heat until sizzling. Add the onions and cook for 1 minute, or until tender. Stir in the flour and cook, stirring constantly with a wooden spoon, for 3 minutes.

step 2. Measure the reserved tuna liquid and add enough milk to make 1 cup liquid. Add this liquid to the onion mixture and bring to a boil, whisking constantly just until slightly thickened. Remove from the heat.

step 3. Meanwhile, cook the potatoes and garlic in an extra-large saucepan of boiling salted water until completely tender but not mushy, about 8 minutes; drain. Mash the potatoes until smooth and lump-free. Stir the mashed potatoes into the sauce until well combined. Gently stir in the tuna chunks, rosemary, chives, salt, and pepper. Taste and adjust the seasoning, if necessary.

step 4. Spoon the tuna mixture into a 10-inch glass pie pan. Roll out the pastry to form a 10-inch circle and place it over the tuna mixture. Trim the pastry even with the rim of the pan. Seal the edges. Cut steam vents and cut out shapes such as fish from the dough trimmings to decorate the top of the crust, if desired. Refrigerate for 30 minutes, then brush lightly with milk.

step 5. Preheat the oven to 375° F.

step 6. Bake the pie for 40 to 45 minutes, or until the top is golden and the filling is hot. Cut into wedges and serve hot.

new-potato omelet *with* tuna *and* asparagus

MAKES 6 TO 8 SERVINGS ➤◄

1 pound unpeeled small, red-skinned potatoes, cut into large chunks

8 ounces asparagus, trimmed, and cut into thirds

About 2 tablespoons fruity olive oil

Salt and freshly ground black pepper

1 can (about 6 ounces) solid light tuna packed in olive oil, well drained and broken into large chunks

12 ounces cherry tomatoes, stemmed and halved, or quartered, if large

6 large eggs (preferably organic)

$1/4$ cup snipped fresh chives or green onion tops

This one-skillet Spanish-style brunch omelet begins with extra-virgin olive oil, tiny new potatoes, crunchy green asparagus, cherry tomatoes, and chives. The beaten eggs are added and cooked briefly, then the omelet is popped under the broiler until nicely browned on top. The omelet is also delicious made with peeled baking potatoes.

PREPARATION

step 1. Cook the potatoes in a medium saucepan of boiling salted water just until tender, about 6 minutes. Immediately add the asparagus and cook for 1 minute; drain well.

step 2. Heat the olive oil in a large, heavy, nonstick oven-proof skillet over high heat. Add the potatoes and asparagus, sprinkle with salt and pepper to taste, and cook for 5 minutes or until the vegetables are lightly golden. Add the tuna and tomatoes and cook for 1 minute.

step 3. Beat the eggs until well blended and pour them over the ingredients in the pan. Sprinkle with the chives, salt, and pepper. Reduce the heat to medium-low and cook for 4 to 5 minutes, or just until the eggs are set but the top is still moist.

step 4. Meanwhile, preheat the broiler. Place the pan under the broiler for 2 minutes, or just until the omelet is lightly golden. Remove from the oven and sprinkle with a little salt. Slice into wedges and serve at once.

secret-ingredient cheese soufflé

MAKES 4 TO 6 SERVINGS

---

4 tablespoons unsalted butter

$1/2$ cup freshly grated Parmesan cheese

1 big, fat garlic clove, chopped

$1/2$ medium red bell pepper, seeded, deribbed, and diced

4 green onions, including the green tops, chopped

3 tablespoons all-purpose flour

$1^{1}/_{4}$ cups milk

1 tablespoon Dijon mustard

$1/2$ teaspoon dry mustard

$1/2$ teaspoon dried thyme

$1/2$ teaspoon salt, plus a pinch

Freshly ground black pepper

$1/8$ teaspoon cayenne pepper

2 tablespoons sour cream

$1/2$ cup (2 ounces) shredded imported Gruyère or Swiss cheese

1 can (about 6 ounces) solid or chunk light tuna packed in oil, well drained and broken into small chunks

4 egg yolks

5 egg whites

Adding a tin of tuna to a cheese soufflé mixture gives the soufflé a much more interesting flavor—and no one will ever guess the secret ingredient. Terrific for a late breakfast or brunch, this savory soufflé is good served with plenty of country bread and chutney. And don't forget the Bloody Marys.

PREPARATION

step 1. Preheat the oven to 350° F. Coat the inside of a 2-quart porcelain soufflé dish with 1 tablespoon of the butter. Dust with 2 tablespoons of the Parmesan cheese. Using kitchen twine, tie a collar of buttered, double-thickness parchment paper around the outside of the soufflé dish. The top should extend 3 inches above the edge of the dish.

step 2. Melt the remaining 3 tablespoons butter in a heavy, medium saucepan over medium heat. Add the garlic, bell pepper, and green onions and cook for 2 minutes, or until tender. Add the flour and cook, stirring constantly with a wooden spoon, for 3 minutes. Don't let the mixture brown (reduce the heat if necessary). Add

the milk and bring the mixture just to a boil, whisking constantly; immediately remove from the heat. Stir in the Dijon and dry mustards, thyme, the $1/2$ teaspoon salt, black pepper to taste, the cayenne, sour cream, Gruyère, remaining Parmesan cheese, and tuna. Let cool slightly, then stir in the egg yolks. Transfer the mixture to a large bowl. (The soufflé can be made ahead to this point, the surface covered with plastic wrap pressed onto it to prevent a skin from forming, and stored in the refrigerator for several hours before cooking.)

step 3. Bring the soufflé mixture to room temperature before proceeding. In a large bowl of an electric mixer, beat the egg whites with a pinch of salt until stiff, glossy peaks form. Using a rubber spatula, fold 1 cup of the mixture into the cheese sauce to lighten it, then gently fold in the remaining egg whites just until combined. Transfer to the prepared soufflé dish and bake for 45 to 55 minutes, or until firm and golden brown. (If necessary, you may turn off the oven—but don't open the door!—and let the soufflé set for another 10 minutes—but no longer.) Serve at once, using 2 serving spoons.

tuna quiche *with* broccoli *and* sweet red pepper

MAKES 8 SERVINGS

1 sheet frozen puff pastry (half of a 17-ounce package), thawed

5 large eggs

2 cups heavy cream

1/2 teaspoon salt

1/4 teaspoon freshly ground black pepper

1/8 teaspoon freshly grated nutmeg

1 tablespoon unsalted butter

1 medium onion, chopped

1 cup coarsely diced red bell pepper

2 cups small broccoli florets

1 can (about 6 ounces) solid light tuna packed in olive oil, well drained and broken into large chunks

1 tablespoon dried oregano

1 1/2 cups (about 6 ounces) shredded imported Gruyère cheese

Quick and simple, this savory quiche makes a satisfying lunch or supper. Bits of bright red pepper and green broccoli enhance the filling, adding color and crunch. Chunks of meaty tuna make the quiche more substantial, and packaged puff pastry makes it easy on the cook. Sautéed sliced mushrooms would also be delicious added to the vegetable mix. Or, try tuna with artichoke hearts and tomatoes instead of broccoli. Quiche is best served the day it is made. You can also bake this quiche in tiny tartlet shells (adjusting the cooking time accordingly) to serve as hors d'oeuvres.

PREPARATION

step 1. Preheat the oven to 375° F. Line a baking sheet with aluminum foil.

step 2. Roll the puff pastry out on a lightly floured surface to a 13-inch square. Line a 10-inch pie pan with the pastry and trim it to leave a 1-inch overhang. Fold the pastry under to make a high rim. Set aside.

step 3. Whisk the eggs, heavy cream, salt, pepper, and nutmeg together in a medium bowl until well blended. Set aside.

step 4. Melt the butter in a large, heavy, nonstick skillet over medium-high heat until sizzling. Add the onion, red pepper, and broccoli and cook for 2 minutes, or just until the vegetables are crisp-tender.

step 5. Spread the mixture over the pastry shell and sprinkle with salt and pepper. Top with the tuna chunks and pour the egg mixture over. Sprinkle with the oregano and shredded cheese.

step 6. Place the pie on the prepared baking sheet and bake for 45 to 50 minutes, or just until firm and a knife inserted into the center comes out clean; don't overcook or the custard may curdle. Let cool for 30 minutes before serving. Serve warm or at room temperature.

farfalle *with* tuna, lemon, *and* caper sauce

MAKES 4 SERVINGS ◂►

12 ounces farfalle (bow-tie pasta)

1 can (about 6 ounces) solid light tuna packed in olive oil, well drained

1 big, fat garlic clove, minced or put through a garlic press

Grated zest of 2 medium lemons

$^1/_4$ cup fresh lemon juice

$^1/_2$ cup fruity olive oil

$^1/_2$ teaspoon salt

Freshly ground black pepper

$^3/_4$ cup Kalamata olives, unpitted or pitted

$^1/_4$ cup drained capers

1 large ($^1/_2$ pound) ripe tomato, seeded and coarsely chopped, or 8 ounces cherry tomatoes, halved

$^1/_2$ cup fresh flat-leaf parsley, chopped

PREPARATION

It's amazing how a few simple pantry staples can create a sauce so superb and yet so simple to make—and it doesn't even need cooking! I've been serving this "instant" pasta dish for many years to last-minute dinner guests and it has never failed to garner praise. All that's needed to round out the meal is some crusty bread and, perhaps, a green salad. Other pasta shapes I use are conchiglie rigate (medium shells), rigatoni, and penne rigate. Before you toss the hot pasta with the sauce ingredients, be sure everything is at room temperature. If serving this sauce in cool weather, simply warm all of the sauce ingredients in a nonreactive skillet before tossing with the pasta.

step 1. Cook the pasta in a large pot of boiling salted water until al dente.

step 2. Meanwhile, place the tuna in a pasta serving bowl and break it into large chunks. Add the garlic, lemon zest, lemon juice, olive oil, salt, pepper to taste, olives, capers, and tomato. Gently stir to combine.

step 3. Drain the pasta well and immediately toss it with the sauce in the bowl. Sprinkle with parsley and serve at once. Pass the pepper mill.

tuna, roasted red pepper, *and* caper pizza

MAKES ONE 14-INCH PIZZA ➤

pizza dough

1 envelope (¹/₄ ounce) active dry yeast

¹/₄ teaspoon sugar

³/₄ cup lukewarm water

1³/₄ cups bread flour or unbleached all-purpose flour

¹/₂ teaspoon salt

pizza topping

Fruity olive oil for coating and drizzling

2 teaspoons dried oregano

2 cups (8 ounces) shredded Monterey Jack or whole-milk mozzarella cheese

1 can (about 6 ounces) solid light tuna packed in olive oil, well drained and broken into large chunks

1 medium red bell pepper, roasted, peeled, and cut into thick julienne (see page 73)

2 tablespoons drained capers

20 Kalamata olives, unpitted or pitted

1 big, fat garlic clove, finely chopped

Salt and freshly ground black pepper

2 tablespoons freshly grated Parmesan cheese

I invented this tuna-topped pizza over a dozen years ago when I was writing my first pizza cookbook. I had previously created a pasta sauce with tuna, zesty capers, and other Mediterranean flavorings, and I felt sure the ingredients would be equally scrumptious on a pizza. I was right! Go ahead and use bottled roasted red pepper and Greek black olives, if you must. But if you make this pizza with the best tuna packed in olive oil, Kalamata olives purchased from a Greek or Italian grocer or the supermarket deli counter, homemade pizza dough, and home-roasted red pepper, the result will be one of the finest pizzas you've ever tasted.

PREPARATION

step 1. To make the pizza dough: Stir the yeast and sugar together with the warm water in a 1-cup measuring cup. Set aside for 10 minutes, or until foamy. Stir again.

step 2. Meanwhile, combine the flour and salt in a food processor or large bowl. With the machine running, pour the yeast mixture through the feed tube and process until the dough forms a ball, about 10 to 20 seconds. Or, pour the yeast mixture into the bowl and knead until combined. Turn the dough out onto a lightly floured surface (the dough will be a little sticky). Knead a few times, dusting with a bit of flour at this point only if the dough is still too sticky. Put the dough in a large bowl and cover the bowl tightly with plastic wrap. Let rise at room temperature for about 1 hour, or until doubled. You can also refrigerate the dough, well covered, for several hours or overnight.

VARIATIONS

step 3. Preheat the oven to 500° F. Lightly coat a 14-inch, heavy black pizza pan with olive oil.

step 4. Roll the dough out on a lightly floured surface into a 14-inch circle and place it on the prepared pan. (If the dough contracts while you're rolling, let it stand for 10 minutes before rolling it out again.) Brush the dough lightly with olive oil to cover completely.

step 5. Sprinkle 1 teaspoon of the dried oregano over the dough, leaving a $1/2$-inch border. Top with the cheese, then the tuna chunks, roasted red pepper, capers, and olives. Sprinkle with the garlic, the remaining 1 teaspoon oregano, a little salt, and a few grindings of pepper. Drizzle with a little olive oil.

step 6. Bake for 5 to 10 minutes, or just until the crust is golden and the cheese is bubbly. Remove the pan from the oven and sprinkle with the Parmesan cheese. Cut into wedges and serve hot.

note. If pressed for time, instead of homemade dough use two 8-inch pita breads and bake on a large, heavy baking sheet lined with aluminum foil.

to *make a* **tex-mex tuna pizza**

Top the pizza dough base with shredded Monterey jack cheese, diced fresh tomato, chopped garlic, tuna chunks, jalapeño peppers, oregano, and chopped fresh cilantro.

for *a* **tuna and bacon pizza**

Top the pizza dough base with shredded mozzarella cheese, coarsely crumbled bacon, diced fresh tomato, tuna chunks, dried oregano, and chopped garlic.

for *a* **greek tuna pizza**

Top the pizza dough base with half crumbled feta and half shredded mozzarella cheese, diced fresh tomato, Kalamata olives, chopped garlic, sliced red onion, tuna chunks, and dried oregano.

for *a* **mediterranean tuna pizza**

Top the pizza dough base with fontina cheese, marinated artichoke hearts, chopped garlic, tuna chunks, diced fresh tomato, dried oregano, and chopped fresh rosemary leaves.

savory tuna-stuffed red peppers

MAKES 3 TO 6 SERVINGS

3 extra-large red bell peppers (about 8 ounces each), halved lengthwise, keeping stems intact, and seeded

1 can (about 6 ounces) solid light tuna packed in olive oil, well drained and broken into large chunks

6 to 8 anchovy fillets, chopped

2 ripe, medium tomatoes, seeded and coarsely chopped

18 Kalamata olives, pitted and very coarsely chopped

3 tablespoons drained capers

1 big, fat garlic clove, minced or put through a garlic press

1/2 cup dry bread crumbs

2 tablespoons finely chopped fresh flat-leaf parsley, plus extra for garnish

1/4 teaspoon salt

Freshly ground black pepper

1/4 cup fruity olive oil, plus extra for serving

Fabulous sweet red peppers are filled with robust Mediterranean flavors: anchovies, olives, capers, tuna, and tomatoes. I like to serve these with crusty bread and a simple green salad. They're also perfectly at home as hearty starters or snacks, or even as a side dish. Don't even think of omitting the anchovies, they're essential—they impart a wonderful flavor to the filling.

PREPARATION

step 1. Preheat the oven to 450° F. Lightly oil the bottom of a 9-by-13-inch glass baking dish or similar dish just large enough to hold the peppers snugly.

step 2. Drop the bell peppers into a large pot of boiling water and simmer for 3 minutes. Using tongs, transfer them to a colander, upside down, to drain. Arrange the peppers, cut side up, in the prepared baking dish.

step 3. Gently combine the tuna, anchovies, tomatoes, olives, capers, garlic, bread crumbs, parsley, salt, and pepper to taste in a medium bowl.

step 4. Spoon the tuna mixture into the peppers and drizzle them with the olive oil. Bake, uncovered, for 20 minutes, or until the stuffing is hot and slightly crusty on top and the peppers are lightly charred in several places. Serve hot or at room temperature sprinkled with parsley. Pass a bottle of fruity olive oil for each person to drizzle over the peppers to taste.

tuna creole

MAKES ABOUT 6 SERVINGS ➤◀

10 bacon slices (Oscar Mayer brand)

1 large onion, chopped

1 celery stalk, finely chopped

1 medium-large green bell pepper, seeded and diced

1 tablespoon all-purpose flour

1 can (28 ounces) tomatoes (not packed with added purée), undrained

1 bay leaf

1 cup homemade chicken stock or canned broth

1 teaspoon sugar

1 teaspoon dried basil

1/2 teaspoon dried thyme

1/2 teaspoon salt

1/4 teaspoon cayenne pepper

1/4 teaspoon coarsely ground black pepper

1 teaspoon Tabasco sauce, plus extra for serving

2 cans (about 6 ounces each) solid light tuna packed in olive oil, well drained and broken into large chunks

Hot cooked rice for serving

Chopped green onion tops for garnish

Chopped flat-leaf parsley for garnish

PREPARATION

Tuna makes a terrific—and inexpensive—stand-in for more expensive seafood entrées made with shrimp or crab, which means we can enjoy these dishes more often, especially when the budget is tight. This is my take on the classic shrimp Creole, in which tuna is combined with a cayenne-spiked tomato sauce and served over mounds of steaming white rice. If you're tempted—as I was—to substitute a sweet red pepper for the green pepper, just remember it's the traditional green pepper that gives the dish that true Creole taste and color. Not only that, an authentic Creole sauce would have at least double the amount of cayenne and black pepper, along with a generous amount of ground white pepper—so turn up the heat if you dare!

step 1. Cook the bacon until crisp in a large, heavy, nonstick skillet over medium-high heat. Using tongs, transfer the bacon to a paper towel–lined plate to drain, leaving 1/4 cup of the bacon fat in the pan.

step 2. Add the onion, celery, and green pepper to the pan and cook for 4 minutes, or until the vegetables are tender. Reduce the heat to medium, add the flour, and cook, stirring constantly with a wooden spoon, for 3 minutes. Add the tomatoes, bay leaf, chicken stock, sugar, basil, thyme, salt, cayenne, black pepper, and Tabasco sauce. Bring to a boil over high heat. Reduce the heat and simmer for 20 minutes, or until slightly thickened. Just before serving, add the tuna and cook for 1 minute, or until heated through. Discard the bay leaf. Serve over hot rice in shallow bowls. Coarsely crumble the bacon and sprinkle it over each serving. Garnish generously with the green onion tops and parsley. Serve at once and pass the Tabasco sauce.

tuna hash *with* fried eggs

MAKES 4 TO 6 SERVINGS ━◄

2 pounds (about 4 large) baking potatoes, peeled and cut into $1/2$-inch dice

$1/4$ cup ($1/2$ stick) unsalted butter
or canola oil

1 big, fat garlic clove, chopped

1 large onion, chopped

1 large red bell pepper, seeded,
deribbed, and diced

1 can (about 6 ounces) solid light
tuna packed in olive oil, well drained
and broken into large chunks

$1/2$ teaspoon salt

$1/8$ teaspoon cayenne pepper

Freshly ground black pepper

2 large green onions, including
green tops, chopped

Fried or poached eggs

PREPARATION

Rarely do I have leftover corned beef to make hash for Sunday breakfast or brunch, so often canned tuna comes to the rescue. In this recipe, the tuna is cooked with diced potatoes, onions, and bright red pepper, but you can replace the red pepper with diced oven-roasted beets to tint everything pink, and add a couple of tablespoons of horseradish to heat things up a bit. The hash is, of course, topped with fried or poached eggs. Serve with toast and tall glasses of ice-cold orange juice whipped until frothy in the blender.

step 1. Boil the potatoes in a large saucepan of boiling salted water for 5 minutes, or just until tender. Drain well and let cool. You may prepare the potatoes up to this point, cover, and refrigerate for several hours or up to overnight.

step 2. Melt the butter (or heat the oil) in a large, heavy, cast-iron or nonstick skillet over medium-high heat until sizzling. Add the garlic, onion, and bell pepper and cook for 2 minutes, or just until the vegetables are tender and the onion is golden. Add the potatoes, tuna, salt, cayenne, black pepper to taste, and green onions and cook, pressing with a spatula to compress the hash, for 5 minutes, or just until the potatoes are golden brown and crispy. Turn over and cook for another 5 minutes, or until golden brown and crisp. Divide among 4 to 6 warmed plates and top with perfectly fried or poached eggs. Serve at once.

classy tuna noodle casserole

MAKES 4 TO 6 SERVINGS

$^1/_4$ cup ($^1/_2$ stick) unsalted butter

2 big, fat garlic cloves, chopped

Grated zest of 2 large lemons

2 cups fresh bread crumbs made from good-quality sourdough or French bread (including crusts)

$^1/_2$ teaspoon salt

1 cup heavy cream

$^1/_4$ cup fresh lemon juice

12 ounces dried fettuccine (preferably De Cecco brand)

1 pound ripe tomatoes, seeded and coarsely diced

1 can (about 6 ounces) solid light tuna packed in olive oil, well drained and broken into large chunks

$^1/_2$ cup freshly grated Parmesan cheese

Freshly ground black pepper

$^1/_4$ cup fresh basil or flat-leaf parsley, chopped

Lemon wedges for serving (optional)

Say goodbye to the canned-mushroom-soup sauce and mushy, overcooked macaroni of yesteryear! Here, fettuccine and tuna are suffused with a luscious, freshly made cream sauce with lots of tangy lemon that's balanced by the delicate flavor of Parmesan cheese and brightened by red tomatoes, elevating the humble tuna-macaroni casserole to casual company's-coming fare that doesn't even need baking. But don't worry—this "upscale" version keeps its comforting, kid-friendly qualities, and it's just as easy to make as the original (well, almost).

PREPARATION

step 1. Melt the butter in a large, heavy, nonstick or nonreactive skillet over medium-high heat until sizzling. Add the garlic and cook for several seconds. Add half of the lemon zest and the bread crumbs and cook, stirring constantly, for 4 minutes, or until golden and crisp; watch carefully, as they can burn very easily. Remove from the heat, sprinkle with a scant $^1/_4$ teaspoon of the salt, and transfer to a plate. Wipe the skillet clean with a paper towel.

step 2. Combine the heavy cream, the remaining lemon zest, and the lemon juice in the same skillet over high heat, bring to a boil, and cook for 3 minutes, or just until slightly thickened; don't overthicken. Remove from the heat.

step 3. Meanwhile, cook the pasta in a large pot of boiling salted water until al dente. Drain well and add to the sauce in the skillet over medium heat. Add the tomatoes, tuna, Parmesan cheese, the remaining $^1/_4$ teaspoon salt, pepper to taste, and basil and gently toss with the sauce to combine. Continue cooking just until heated through. Divide the pasta among 4 to 6 warmed shallow bowls or plates and sprinkle with the toasted bread crumbs. Serve with lemon wedges, if desired, and pass the pepper mill.

tuna tetrazzini

MAKES 6 TO 8 SERVINGS

4 tablespoons unsalted butter

10 ounces medium-sized mushrooms, thinly sliced

2 big, fat garlic cloves, chopped

$^1/_4$ cup all-purpose flour

$2^1/_4$ cups homemade chicken stock or canned broth

1 cup heavy cream

3 tablespoons medium-dry sherry

$^1/_2$ teaspoon salt

Freshly ground black pepper

2 cans (about 6 ounces each) solid light tuna packed in olive oil, well drained and broken into large chunks

8 ounces spaghetti (preferably De Cecco brand)

$^1/_2$ cup freshly grated Parmesan cheese

Named after the Italian opera singer Luisa Tetrazzini, this popular fifties classic is typically prepared with chicken or leftover turkey in a sherry-flavored mushroom cream sauce. In this pleasing rendition, meaty tuna is substituted for the chicken.

PREPARATION

step 1. Melt 1 tablespoon of the butter in a large, heavy, nonstick skillet over high heat until sizzling. Add the mushrooms and cook for 3 minutes, or until beginning to brown; add the garlic and cook for several seconds or until tender. Remove to a plate.

step 2. Melt the remaining 3 tablespoons butter in the same skillet over medium heat. Add the flour and cook, stirring constantly with a wooden spoon, for 3 minutes. Add the chicken stock, heavy cream, sherry, salt, and pepper to taste and bring to a boil, whisking constantly; remove from the heat. Add the mushroom mixture, including the accumulated juices, to the sauce in the skillet. Gently stir in the tuna chunks and set aside.

step 3. Preheat the oven to 350° F. Lightly butter a 9-by-13-inch glass baking dish.

step 4. Cook the spaghetti in a large pot of boiling salted water until al dente. Drain well. Put the spaghetti in the prepared baking dish. Pour the mushroom-tuna sauce over the spaghetti and gently lift it with 2 forks to distribute the mixture. Sprinkle the top with the Parmesan cheese.

step 5. Bake the casserole for 20 to 25 minutes, or until the top is pale golden and the casserole is hot and bubbly; don't overbake or the sauce will overthicken. Serve at once and pass the pepper mill.

tuna stroganoff

MAKES 4 SERVINGS ◗◗

1 tablespoon unsalted butter

2 big, fat garlic cloves, chopped

3³/₄ cups water

8 ounces extra-wide egg noodles

¹/₂ cup coarsely snipped chives or chopped green onion tops, plus extra for garnish

1 can (about 6 ounces) solid light tuna packed in olive oil, well drained and broken into large chunks

³/₄ cup sour cream

1 cup (4 ounces) shredded extra-sharp Cheddar cheese, plus extra for garnish

¹/₂ teaspoon salt

Freshly ground black pepper

Lemon wedges for serving

PREPARATION

Packages of instant tuna "helper" dinners abound at the supermarket, so I thought it would be fun to concoct a homemade version. This is almost as easy as the packaged version (it's a one-skillet meal), and although I've never tasted the storebought stuff, I know this has to taste soooo much better made from scratch with real garlic, cheese, sour cream, and fresh chives. And even though this is an "everyday entrée," don't let that stop you from using really good aged Cheddar. It adds a nice tangy note to this delicious, homey dish. All that's needed is a crunchy green salad on the side and you've got a great meal. It is essential to use a 12-inch skillet for this recipe.

step 1. Melt the butter in a 12-inch, heavy, nonstick skillet over high heat until sizzling. Add the garlic and cook for several seconds, or until it just begins to turn golden.

step 2. Add the water, egg noodles, and chives and bring to a boil over high heat. Cook the noodles, stirring occasionally, uncovered, for 6 to 7 minutes, or until about ¹/₄ inch of water remains in the skillet. (The water is needed to make the sauce. If there is too much liquid in the pan, the sauce will be thin and bland; too little and it will be gloppy.) Remove the pan from the heat and gently stir in the tuna, sour cream, cheese, salt, and pepper to taste until combined. Return to the heat to warm through. Serve at once, in warmed shallow bowls with lemon wedges. Garnish each serving with shredded cheese and chives.

portuguese rice *and* tuna casserole

MAKES ABOUT 6 SERVINGS ⚓

6 bacon slices (Oscar Mayer brand), cut crosswise into $^1/_2$-inch pieces

2 big, fat garlic cloves, chopped

4 large green onions, chopped, white and green tops kept separated

$^1/_8$ teaspoon cayenne pepper

2 cups long-grain rice

3 cups homemade chicken stock or canned broth

$^1/_2$ teaspoon salt

Freshly ground black pepper

1 can (about 6 ounces) solid light tuna packed in olive oil, well drained and broken into large chunks

$^3/_4$ cup roasted red peppers, bottled or homemade (see page 73), very coarsely chopped

$^3/_4$ cup Kalamata olives, pitted and halved

$^1/_2$ cup fresh flat-leaf parsley, chopped

Grated zest of 1 large lemon

Lemon wedges for serving

PREPARATION

Simply prepared, this colorful and piquant pilau is seasoned with the zest of lemon, garlic, bacon, and cayenne and combined with tuna, black olives, and roasted red pepper. Make sure to serve this dish with plenty of juicy lemon wedges.

step 1. Cook the bacon in a heavy, large saucepan over medium-high heat, just until crisp. Leaving the bacon fat in the pan, add the garlic, the white part of the green onions, and the cayenne and cook for 1 minute, or until tender. Stir in the rice, then add the chicken stock, salt, and pepper to taste and bring to a boil. Reduce the heat to medium-low, cover, and cook for 20 minutes, or until the liquid is absorbed and the rice is tender.

step 2. Gently stir in the tuna, roasted red peppers, olives, parsley, green onion tops, and lemon zest. Serve hot with lemon wedges.

risotto *with* tuna *and* tomatoes

MAKES 4 TO 6 SERVINGS ➛

About 5 cups homemade chicken stock or canned broth

2 tablespoons unsalted butter

2 tablespoons fruity olive oil

2 big, fat garlic cloves, chopped

1 medium onion, chopped

12 ounces (1²/₃ cups) Arborio rice

¹/₄ cup dry white vermouth or chicken stock or canned broth

12 ounces ripe tomatoes, seeded and chopped, or cherry tomatoes, halved

1 can (about 6 ounces) solid light tuna packed in olive oil, well drained and broken into large chunks

¹/₄ cup freshly grated Parmesan cheese

¹/₂ teaspoon salt

Freshly ground black pepper

¹/₄ cup fresh flat-leaf parsley, chopped

Risotto variations are endless and endlessly pleasing. Here, tuna and tomato commingle with Arborio rice to create an excellent, easygoing entrée that's pure comfort food, yet good enough to serve to good friends as an informal dinner. I don't understand why so many cooks seem afraid to make this wonderful dish. I find it very relaxing, glass of wine in hand, to stand at the stove stirring the rice and watching as it slowly coalesces into a delicious, creamy masterpiece. A tart green salad, more wine, and a fresh fruit dessert are all you need to complete a totally satisfying meal.

PREPARATION

step 1. Bring the chicken stock to a simmer in a medium saucepan over high heat. Reduce the heat to low.

step 2. Melt the butter with the oil in a large, heavy, non-reactive saucepan over medium-high heat until sizzling. Add the garlic and onion and cook for 1 minute, or until

tender. Add the rice and stir to coat with the butter and oil. Add the vermouth and stir constantly until most of the liquid is absorbed, about 1 minute. Reduce the heat to medium, add ¹/₂ cup of the hot chicken stock, and stir until most is absorbed. Repeat this process for about 20 minutes, adding the stock ¹/₂ cup at a time, stirring frequently, and tasting toward the end of cooking until the rice is creamy but slightly al dente. (Not all the stock may be needed.)

step 3. Gently stir in the tomatoes, tuna, Parmesan, salt, pepper to taste, and parsley and cook for several seconds, until heated through. Remove the pan from the heat and serve at once in warmed shallow bowls.

VARIATIONS

to *make* extra-lemony tuna risotto

Replace the tomatoes and parsley with the grated zest of 1 large lemon, 2 tablespoons fresh lemon juice, ¹/₄ cup drained capers, and a sprinkling of snipped fresh chives·

fried rice *with* tuna *and* crispy bacon

MAKES 4 TO 6 SERVINGS ➥

3 cups water

2 cups long-grain rice

³/₄ teaspoon salt

6 bacon slices (Oscar Mayer brand)

2 tablespoons canola oil

1 big, fat garlic clove, chopped

1 tablespoon finely chopped fresh ginger

¹/₂ cup coarsely snipped fresh chives or chopped green onion tops

1 cup frozen tiny peas

1 can (about 6 ounces) solid light tuna packed in olive oil, well drained and broken into large chunks

2 tablespoons soy sauce (preferably Kikkoman brand)

Rice is eminently receptive to almost any ingredient, and this stir-fried rice with tuna, crisp bacon, and green peas is a perfect example. It's a quick-and-easy one-bowl meal that's fun to eat with chopsticks, and a side dish of stir-fried Chinese vegetables rounds out the meal nicely. The secret to perfect fried rice is to use cold cooked long-grain rice (never converted or instant). You may use cold leftover rice, or cook it ahead, cover, and refrigerate it for about 2 hours or as long as overnight before using. When cooking rice, ignore the package directions, which usually call for too much liquid and result in soggy, gummy rice.

PREPARATION

step 1. Bring the water to a boil in a heavy, medium saucepan over high heat. Stir in the rice and ¹/₄ teaspoon of the salt. Reduce the heat to medium-low, cover, and cook for 20 minutes, or until the liquid is absorbed and the rice is tender. Remove the pan from the heat, remove the cover, and fluff it with a fork. Let the rice stand, uncovered, until completely cooled. Transfer to a bowl, cover, and refrigerate for at least 2 hours before using.

step 2. Fry the bacon in a large, heavy, nonstick skillet or wok over medium-high heat until crisp. Using tongs, transfer the bacon to a paper towel–lined plate to drain, leaving the bacon fat in the pan. Coarsely crumble the bacon and set aside.

step 3. Add the canola oil to the bacon fat in the pan and heat until very hot. Add the garlic, ginger, chives, and peas and cook for 30 seconds. Add the rice, breaking up any lumps with your hands before adding, then add the tuna and the remaining ¹/₂ teaspoon salt, and stir-fry for 1 to 2 minutes, or until the rice is heated through. Add the soy sauce, toss until combined, then sprinkle with the bacon and toss again. Serve at once.

rigatoni *with* tuna *and* artichoke sauce

MAKES 4 TO 6 SERVINGS ➤◄

½ cup fruity olive oil

1 big, fat garlic clove, minced or put through a garlic press

1 can (about 6 ounces) solid light tuna packed in olive oil, well drained and broken into large chunks

2 jars (6 ounces each) marinated artichoke hearts, drained and very coarsely chopped

½ teaspoon dried oregano

¼ teaspoon red pepper flakes

Grated zest of 1 medium lemon

1 tablespoon fresh lemon juice

½ teaspoon salt

Freshly ground black pepper

12 ounces rigatoni (preferably De Cecco brand)

¼ cup fresh flat-leaf parsley, chopped

PREPARATION

Whenever the subject of artichokes comes up, my mother never fails to tell me she thinks they're highly overrated. She may not like them much, but I do, and I always try to have marinated, canned, and frozen varieties on hand for spur-of-the-moment dishes like this one. This pleasing no-cook pasta sauce is infinitely adaptable—you can add some black olives, coarsely diced sun-dried tomatoes, or roasted red pepper (or all three) for even more pizzazz. If serving this sauce in cool weather, simply warm all of the sauce ingredients in a nonreactive skillet before tossing with the pasta.

step 1. Gently combine the olive oil, garlic, tuna, artichoke hearts, oregano, red pepper flakes, lemon zest, lemon juice, salt, and pepper to taste in a pasta serving bowl.

step 2. Cook the pasta in a large pot of boiling salted water until al dente. Drain well and add to the sauce in the bowl. Toss until combined, sprinkle with parsley, and serve at once.

eggplant *and* tuna gratin

MAKES 6 TO 8 SERVINGS 🐟

3 pounds medium eggplants, unpeeled and cut crosswise into $1/4$-inch-thick rounds

Salt for sprinkling, plus $1/2$ teaspoon

Fruity olive oil for brushing plus 2 tablespoons

2 big, fat garlic cloves, chopped

1 large onion, chopped

1 pound cherry tomatoes, stemmed

$1/4$ cup fresh flat-leaf parsley, chopped

$1/4$ cup fresh basil leaves, chopped

2 cans (about 6 ounces each) solid light tuna packed in olive oil, well drained and broken into large chunks

Freshly ground black pepper

1 teaspoon dried oregano

$1/2$ cup freshly grated Parmesan cheese, plus extra for sprinkling

12 ounces (about 3 cups) shredded Monterey Jack cheese

Eggplant is one of my favorite vegetables—and it's one of the most versatile vegetables on the planet. It's featured in cuisines around the world, from Asia to the Mediterranean to the Middle East. I rarely peel eggplant as I like the deep purple skin for both its appearance and taste. I also don't bother to salt eggplant to remove excess moisture or bitterness. If you choose beautiful, fresh eggplants with glossy, taut purple skin, it usually isn't necessary. To check for bitterness, I taste a tiny raw piece. This earthy eggplant and tuna gratin can be assembled ahead, covered, and refrigerated until baking.

PREPARATION

step 1. Preheat the boiler. Line a broiler pan with aluminum foil and oil the foil well. Arrange one layer of the eggplant on the pan and broil about 3 inches from the heat for about 3 minutes, or until nicely browned. Using tongs, turn the eggplant over and broil for another 3 minutes, or until tender and nicely browned on the second side. Transfer the cooked eggplant to a tray. Repeat to broil the remaining eggplant in the same manner. Sprinkle the eggplant with salt.

step 2. Preheat the oven to 375° F.

step 3. Heat the 2 tablespoons olive oil in a large, heavy, nonstick skillet over high heat. Add the garlic and onion and cook for 1 minute, or until tender. Reduce the heat to medium-high, add the tomatoes, and cook for 10 minutes, or just until the tomatoes are softened. Carefully flatten them with the back of a wooden spoon. Stir in the parsley, basil, tuna, the $1/2$ teaspoon salt, pepper to taste, the oregano, and the Parmesan cheese.

step 4. Lightly oil a 9-by-13-inch glass baking dish. Arrange one layer of eggplant on the bottom. Top with one-third of the tuna mixture, sprinkle with salt and pepper, and one-third of the Monterey Jack cheese. Continue making layers until all the ingredients are used, ending with the cheese.

step 5. Bake the gratin for 20 to 30 minutes, or just until heated through and bubbly; don't overcook. If there is liquid in the pan, let the gratin stand for a few minutes before serving, to allow most of the liquid to be reabsorbed. Sprinkle each serving with a little Parmesan cheese and serve at once.

tuna cakes *with* lime, fresh chives, *and* parsley

MAKES 8 PATTIES

¼ cup mayonnaise

1 large egg

Grated zest of 2 limes

2 tablespoons fresh lime juice

1 teaspoon Worcestershire sauce

½ teaspoon Tabasco sauce

2 cans (about 6 ounces each) solid light tuna packed in olive oil, well drained and broken into large flakes and chunks

$1/3$ cup dry bread crumbs

¼ cup fresh flat-leaf parsley, chopped

½ cup coarsely snipped fresh chives or chopped green onion tops

½ teaspoon salt

Freshly ground black pepper

2 tablespoons unsalted butter

1 tablespoon canola oil

Lime wedges for serving

Crème Fraîche Tartar Sauce (see variation)

All the flavors of crab cakes are combined in these tasty tuna patties. A crunchy salad and a crème fraîche tartar sauce are perfect accompaniments. When combining the ingredients for the tartar sauce, stir as little and as gently as possible to keep the mixture thick (the more you stir, the thinner the sauce becomes).

PREPARATION

step 1. Stir the mayonnaise, egg, lime zest, lime juice, Worcestershire sauce, and Tabasco together in a bowl until combined. Add the tuna, bread crumbs, parsley, chives, salt, and pepper to taste and gently fold the ingredients together. Cover and refrigerate for at least 1 hour or up to 4 hours; the mixture will thicken.

step 2. Melt the butter with the oil in a large, heavy, nonstick skillet over medium-high heat. Gently form the tuna mixture into 8 patties (don't overhandle; the tuna cakes should just hold their shape), adding them to the pan as you make them. Fry the patties for 2 to 3 minutes on each side, or just until heated through, golden brown, and crisp. (They are quite fragile, so turn them carefully—I use 2 metal spatulas.) Carefully transfer the patties to a paper towel–lined plate to drain briefly, then serve at once with lime wedges and crème fraîche tartar sauce.

VARIATIONS

to *make* **louisiana tuna cakes**

Cook ¼ cup *each* diced red, green, and yellow bell pepper in a little butter until crisp-tender, then gently stir them and $1/8$ teaspoon cayenne into the uncooked tuna cake mixture and proceed with the recipe. Serve with a tartar sauce made by combining $3/4$ cup crème fraîche or sour cream with the zest of 2 limes, $1 1/2$ teaspoons fresh lime juice, ¼ cup snipped fresh chives, 1 tablespoon chopped pickled jalapeños, and 3 tablespoons capers. Keep refrigerated until using.

for **tuna "po' boy" sandwiches**

Make smaller patties using the Louisiana Tuna Cakes variation, and spread some of the tartar sauce on both sides of 4 to 6 halved 5-inch lengths of French bread. Pile on shredded lettuce, add the tuna patties, top with the remaining bread, and serve with plenty of napkins.

tuna à la king

MAKES 4 SERVINGS

2 to 3 tablespoons unsalted butter

1/2 medium red bell pepper, seeded, deribbed, and diced

8 medium-large mushrooms, coarsely chopped

1/2 cup homemade chicken stock or canned broth

1/4 cup dry white vermouth

1 cup heavy cream

1/2 teaspoon salt

Freshly ground black pepper

1 teaspoon fresh lemon juice

1 can (about 6 ounces) solid light tuna packed in olive oil, well drained and broken into large chunks

Hot buttered egg noodles, rice, orzo, or buttered toasted English muffins for serving

2 tablespoons finely chopped fresh flat-leaf parsley for garnish

Heavy cream happens to suit so many fish and sea-food sauces—and tuna is no exception. This popular specialty from the forties and fifties has stood the test of time. And no wonder: it's delicious, it's sooth-ing, and it's worth every calorie! Indulge in a dinner dish like this every once in a while (not every night!) and you shouldn't gain any weight. And, if you enjoy a glass of wine with your meal, as the French do, sup-posedly your heart won't mind the cholesterol, either. Instead of serving it over toast points or patty shells as they did in earlier times, I like to spoon it over buttered egg noodles, rice, orzo, or toasted English muffins. Serve with your favorite green vegetable.

PREPARATION

step 1. Melt 2 tablespoons of the butter in a large, heavy, nonstick skillet over medium-high heat until siz-zling. Add the bell pepper and cook for 2 minutes, or until tender; remove to a plate. Add the mushrooms to the pan (add more butter first if necessary) and cook for 2 minutes, or until tender; remove to the plate with the bell pepper.

step 2. Add the chicken stock and vermouth to the skil-let, bring to a boil, and cook for 3 minutes, or until slightly reduced. Add the heavy cream, salt, and pepper to taste, bring to a boil, and simmer for another 3 minutes, or just until slightly thickened. Reduce the heat to low, add the cooked bell pepper and mushrooms with the accumu-lated juices, the lemon juice, and tuna, and cook for 1 minute, or until heated through.

step 3. Spoon the tuna mixture over the noodles, rice, orzo, or toasted English muffins. Sprinkle each portion with parsley and serve at once.

chicken tonnato

MAKES 4 TO 6 SERVINGS ➤

---

4 skinless, boneless chicken breast halves

2 to 4 cups homemade chicken stock or canned broth

1 cup mayonnaise

1 small can (about 3 ounces) solid light tuna packed in olive oil, well drained

2 to 4 tablespoons fresh lemon juice

8 finely chopped anchovy fillets

3 tablespoons drained capers, plus extra for garnish

Lots of grated lemon zest for garnish

Fresh basil or flat-leaf parsley for garnish

Kalamata olives, pitted and sliced for garnish

PREPARATION

Poached chicken breasts cut into thin "scallops" are swathed in a tangy tuna sauce in a dish reminiscent of Italy's famous *vitello tonnato* (veal with tuna sauce). Ideal for summer entertaining, this dish is served cold and should be made ahead of time. Drizzle the tuna sauce over the chicken just before serving. Sprinkle with capers and garnish with lots of lemon zest, basil leaves, and olives. Serve alfresco with two salads: a crunchy Italian green bean salad and a lemony artichoke salad, along with crusty country bread, a glass of lightly chilled Chardonnay, and a fresh-fruit dessert.

step 1. Put the chicken in a medium saucepan or skillet. Add enough chicken stock to cover. Bring to a boil and immediately reduce the heat to low. Cover and simmer very gently for 10 to 15 minutes, or until the chicken is opaque throughout. Remove from the heat, uncover, and let the chicken cool in the broth.

step 2. Meanwhile, stir the mayonnaise, tuna, lemon juice to taste, and anchovies in a bowl until combined. Stir in the capers. Cover and refrigerate for at least 2 hours or up to 24 hours.

step 3. Drain the chicken and cut it on the diagonal into $1/4$-inch-thick "scallops" and arrange them on a platter. Cover with plastic wrap and refrigerate for at least 2 hours or up to 24 hours.

step 4. Just before serving, spoon some of the tuna sauce over the chicken and generously garnish with capers, lemon zest, basil leaves, and olives. Serve the remaining sauce on the side.

table *of* equivalents

The exact equivalents in the following tables have been rounded for convenience.

liquid/dry measures

U.S.	METRIC
$^1/_4$ teaspoon	1.25 milliliters
$^1/_2$ teaspoon	2.5 milliliters
1 teaspoon	5 milliliters
1 tablespoon (3 teaspoons)	15 milliliters
1 fluid ounce (2 tablespoons)	30 milliliters
$^1/_4$ cup	60 milliliters
$^1/_3$ cup	80 milliliters
$^1/_2$ cup	120 milliliters
1 cup	240 milliliters
1 pint (2 cups)	480 milliliters
1 quart (4 cups, 32 ounces)	960 milliliters
1 gallon (4 quarts)	3.84 liters
1 ounce (by weight)	28 grams
1 pound	454 grams
2.2 pounds	1 kilogram

length

U.S.	METRIC
$^1/_8$ inch	3 millimeters
$^1/_4$ inch	6 millimeters
$^1/_2$ inch	12 millimeters
1 inch	2.5 centimeters

oven temperature

FAHRENHEIT	CELSIUS	GAS
250	120	$^1/_2$
275	140	1
300	150	2
325	160	3
350	180	4
375	190	5
400	200	6
425	220	7
450	230	8
475	240	9
500	260	10